Levit

View

Lessons Voiced from an Extraordinary Journey

Volume I

The Wonder Years

Willie Naulls

Library of Congress Cataloging-in-Publication Data

Naulls, Willie
Levitation's View: Lessons Voiced from an Extraordinary Journey
208 p.

ISBN 0-9763709-0-5

1. Naulls, William D. (Willie)
2. Basketball – Biography
3. Athletics – Philosophy
4. Religion
5. Conduct of Life

Except as noted, Scriptural references use the New International Version of the Holy Bible.

Cover and interior design by Dr. Anne Van de Water Naulls
Cover cartoon figure by Karl Hubenthal, *The Los Angeles Examiner*, 9 March 1956.
Photograph of Willie Naulls on back cover of book and rear inside flap of dust cover by Peter A. Robertson, Father & Daughter Photography, 2001.

Published by Willie Naulls Ministries
Post Office Box 7477
Laguna Niguel, California 92607-7477
willie.naulls@cox.net • www.willienaulls.org

Manufactured in the United States of America
International Standard Book Number:

ISBN 0-9763709-0-5

9 780976 370901   90000

I am thankful to God for this entire expression.

For my wife

Dr. Anne Van de Water Naulls

who is "my found Good Thing" of Proverbs' Truth.

Her loyalty, her love of God and honoring of His
Commandments taught to us by Jesus Christ
is a constant reminder to me that
God really does love me and He really does
honor His Word above all His Name.

To God be the Glory, forever and ever.

Thank you, Anne
I love you as Christ loves our Christian family.

Willie

Table of Contents

Foreword

Writing down the foundational **Lessons** for living that my mother taught me is the passion and sensed duty of my lifetime, all consuming and purposeful. I have prayed for guidance to share my story in a way that will inspire others to introspectively work out their God-created purpose. "Who Am I?" is a question I pray this book will inspire each reader to embrace. Unpacking my stored experiences, sharing the impact my mentors and teachers have had on me, whether positive or negative, and evaluating my contravened trek is an exhilarating opportunity to share with those searching for examples of people who have survived to prosper against great odds.

During my first nine years of life in segregated Dallas, Texas, in the 1930s and early '40s, I learned the importance of developing a strong work ethic from my mother's Biblical teachings. Teachers and coaches in the predominantly White San Pedro, California, school system rewarded my efforts as I continued to mature. I lived the acculturation of American color norms and mores at UCLA and through professional basketball under the integrating force of two coaching legends, UCLA's John Wooden and the Boston Celtics' Red Auerbach. From overt to covert, Blacks and Whites shadow boxed toward gradually releasing selfishly sustained goals for posterity. God used His talent in me as an entrée into cross-cultural growth. I was a combatant immersed in the greater war to supersede the COLOR RACE. This faith declaration has been my venture beyond "seeing to believe" toward

"believing to see."

Through the 1960s, my generation had the greatest opportunity to impact open and fair competition for the first time. Physical success and exposure in sports opened up academic environments and exposed young people covered with Black skin for the first time to the best instruction, facilities and cross-cultural contacts.

From the 1970s, entrepreneurs tap danced around the issue of Race and Skin Color until competition to make money through winning forced the *sage* to the battle's inevitable conclusion: True evaluation of a man or woman is first individual, judging his or her character, talents and performance. That truth surfaced that it is counterproductive to competitive enterprise to ever separate people into the categories of Black and White.

As my life began in poverty and oppression in the ghetto of segregated Dallas, it improved through the freedom of opportunity to work and develop spiritually, mentally and physically in my new integrated community of San Pedro (**WONDER YEARS**), advanced through the environment of open competition at UCLA (**WOODEN YEARS**) which continued into the NBA and Business World (**WORLD YEARS**), was transformed into a new birth when I committed my life to serving in the ministry of Jesus Christ (**WORD YEARS**), and has evolved into a maturing work together with God to inspire youth to work at developing into the full measure of the gifts and talents they were given at birth (**WITNESS YEARS**).

In retrospect, I was never embraced by the

"homeboys" because I did not grow up on the East Side of Los Angeles, under the influence of the two predominantly African American high schools. Instead, I grew up in the governmental projects of San Pedro, where the vast majority of the residents of the town were White. I represent the very few African Americans from the period before Brown v. Board of Education who, at a young age, were thrust out of an all Black world into an all White world – and the fewer still who have survived to prosper. (I believe that professional football Hall of Famer Jim Brown, Olympic Decathlon Champion Rafer Johnson and Harvard Medical School Professor of Orthopædics and Orthopædic Surgeon-in-Chief, Emeritus, of Beth Israel Deaconess Medical Center Augustus A. White, III, M.D., Ph.D., had similar histories.) Because my parents sought a different route for me, I walked the tight rope of two worlds, Black and White, constantly striving to prove my abilities and worth. I benefited from being exposed to the *"better"* public schools, teachers and opportunities offered in socio-economically privileged communities where parents demand that their children be presented with the best opportunities.

A first-team All-City performer in baseball and basketball and captain for two years in each sport in high school, I went on to earn All-America honors under Coach John Wooden at UCLA. As a member of the NBA's New York Knicks, I was honored to be the first African American team captain in integrated professional sports while earning four All-Star berths. I ended my ten year professional career as a three-time World Champion with the Boston Celtics which introduced the first all African American

starting team in the history of integrated professional sports, under Coach Red Auerbach. After
retiring, I launched an entrepreneurial career,
developing several enterprises including take-out
restaurants; a shopping center; companies spe-
cializing in professional contract negotiation and
financial management, executive search, executive
gifts, and residential and commercial real estate
development; a bank; a thrift and loan company;
an automobile dealership; and a non-profit youth
training and development organization.

In the midst of my entrepreneurial pursuits, I
experienced an epiphany with God Almighty. He
called me to ministry, speaking forth this command:

*"Get out of business and better prepare yourself
to minister My Word and tell people what
great things I have done in your life."*

That awesome experience became the moti-
vating moment for me to explore my Purpose
here on earth. Following years of individual study
and formal training, I founded a Christian based
missionary ministry (Willie Naulls Ministries), a
non-denominational church (The Church of
Common Ground), and, most recently, Rising
Stars Christian Academy, which focuses on better
preparing young people of all races through
spiritual, academic and athletic leadership training
and development with the result of maturing
them to live in God's purpose as they prosper to
serve others.

I am married to UCLA School of Medicine
graduate Dr. Anne Van de Water Naulls. Our
four children include Lisa, a professional singer and

graduate of Stanford University and the UCLA Graduate School of Music; Shannon, a UCLA educated computer professional who is married with two children; Jonah, a former UCLA student, currently in the entertainment industry; and Malaika, a University of Florida graduate in Advertising and Business Management, also in the entertainment industry. Anne put her medical career on hold to be wife and mother indeed and available to our children as we stressed their educational, personal and spiritual growth.

For many years I avoided the subject of writing or even talking about my family. Only after God called me to ministry with specific instructions did I get a hint that a retrospective of my life's experiences could be an encouragement to others. I have mentioned in various public expressions that, when I was newly called to ministry, Pastor Jack Hayford encouraged me, prophetically I believe, to write down what God would give me to say. He said to pray about publishing a monthly ministry newsletter, which I did for two years. That experience awakened in me a desire to write down on paper God's grace in my life, and that zeal lives on in me through this book. Mom taught me that the good fruit of a **Lesson** learned is to be shared with others.

My clear and present duty is upon me to write down my experiences, especially as a work to glorify God. I pray that my life story in prose and poetry will motivate those around me of all races to work at becoming the full measure of whom God created them individually to be.

Now I lay me down to sleep
yearning to express my soul does weep
In the depths of my heart I did keep
hurts overflowing – began to seep
Then one morning soon thereafter
so Empowered – my own book crafter

Introductory Ode
My Boyhood's Dilemma

When I was just a little boy
I asked my mother, What will I be?
Will I be safe?
Will I be free?
How often did she say to me

You're no different from any other lad
It's what you choose to be, so be glad
Let the sky be your horizon
unlimited choices for you to *work out*
Be careful not to take on sap sucking
     baggage
that impedes your daily best clout

Deep within Mom's thoughts did dwell
her soul competing, alert to compel
the truth abiding in her heart to foretell
what I desperately needed – to know
     Christ well

Some men confess of visions great
with thoughts of attaining power
suppressing for a pregnant time
the gift of God, **The Endower**

What I want to herein tell
is the Truth surging, purging, competing,
desperately confronting insecurity's
     secrets
to tap the depths of my unknown well

The Wonder Years

From deep within the darkness
of the land of my birth
came God's Light to guide me
through Mom's Lessons' Worth

Bettie Arlene Naulls

"Obedience to God is required.
Judgment by skin color is not of Him inspired."

Bettie Arlene Naulls

The Wonder Years

Tantamount to the holistic development of a child's character and mind and body is a committed teacher of individual **Lessons**. Empathizing, the teacher's character is grounded in inspired purpose to serve his or her pupil. My Mother was that image of a submitted and committed LOVE centered teacher whom I knew to be Super Mom. The **Lessons** she taught me were Spiritual, mental and physical principles to live by that shored up my preparing foundation in the segregated and hostile environments of my youth. From that platform of inner security, I faced every challenge from inside out. Even when I made mistakes in yielding to the lures from outside my inner fort, I knew the right from wrong taught to my inner man by my Mother.

Black skinned folk and White skinned folk,
and all those not of Kin,
have to reckon with **The Maker**
who judges what's within.

Willie

Age 8 years
Dallas, Texas

God Promised –
In the Beginning

In the Beginning
In a place where
life itself seemed forlorn
came of Daily
but by Bettie
Willie Naulls was born.

Roaches greeting
Rats competing
Stench of death every
    where
Hated skin
'cause of color
and the curl in my hair.

Curse of **Promise**
Judgment coming
Lord God bound to
    His Word
woe in conscience
of the bearers
His justice to disturb

Contrite utterance
Strict adherence
to her code was my
    fare
Submissive mode
did my mother
Pledge my life to God's
    care

There's tomorrow
through the sorrow
Faith's blessings will
    to be
through His hope
launched the growing
of my fruit bearing tree

Scream of freedom
Came to witness
sweet milk and honey
    of His will
Purpose molding
Promise unfolding
Growing in under-
    standing still!

Lesson on the Legendary Boogie Man

My Mom always taught when I wanted to learn and could benefit to grow. These Lessons empowered my decisions and molded me into whomever I chose to become. When people who were entrusted with my care did something in my presence contrary to her teachings or attempted to lure me into doing something contrary to what she had taught me, I was empowered to make the choice to do what I knew was right. Standing firm I could make a decision which would honor or dishonor a Lesson that she had taught me to know would be in my best interest. In other words, Bettie A. Naulls' children knew how to act when she was not around.

During one fall day, my brother and I were in the care of a young teenage member of our church whom my mother trusted. She took us for a walk and on the way home we passed a graveyard next to the grammar school I would attend. Our home was diagonally across the school's property from where we were walking, and my brother and I were lagging further and further behind Gladyce who vociferously demanded that we keep up. We ignored her and continued to pick up rocks and hurl them into the graveyard. All of a sudden she stopped, put her hands over her face with her eyes wide open toward the graveyard. She said, "I just saw the *Boogie Man* looking from behind that grave stone and I think he's coming to get you two!" My brother and I leaped in unison on our three-and two-year-old legs respectively toward her as she ran ahead of us increasing the span between with every step. We screamed and cried our way up on the porch at our home and into the safety behind the *hooked* screen door.

I sometimes heard adults in our home passing along what they considered to be very humorous stories. After that day, the one recorded above was included; but this one wasn't very funny to me. Many nights would pass before the Boogie Man would leave me alone – from behind the shadow of a half opened door, or in the unknown in the darkness of an unlit room, or during nighttime walking – with or without my parents. My Mom gave *Gladyce* a lecture about what purpose her tactic of scaring the minds of her two boys served. In a very stern but self controlled voice, she offered, "*Gladyce*, when you have children of your own, don't allow anyone to burden them with fear tactics. Caution and train them in the respect for the potential of evil's wrath. That is healthy for the mind, but fear for fear's sake is only harmful to the souls of children. So don't ever do that to my children again! Do you hear me, *Gladyce*?" she glared in the firmness of love's conviction. "Yes, ma'am, I won't do it again."

Fear is a powerful influence. How important the One who protects you from the many forms of evil. Who is it in my Mom who would die for me, and my safety, and my nurturing, and my benefit, and my growth in knowledge of how to think and do for myself?

It surely was God in Jesus Christ that she spoke into me, whom I did not acknowledge until almost 40 years later.

It is impressive to mouth "There is nothing to fear but fear itself," but more meaningful to children when a parent or guardian is the Vanguard of his or her child's fears from birth and on through the developmental years. The responsibility of presence to consistently walk with and before and behind one's own child promotes healthy stress-free question-answering developing years of the child, when he or she needs it, whether the child is aware of the need or not. Fear is torment! Fear retards growth! Fear impedes understanding of knowledge ingested. Fear is detrimental to all people in all circumstances. Fear does not discriminate by race or color or nationality or gender. Fear comes to steal, to kill, and to destroy. Fear is not a respecter of persons. Fear is taught to children and fear is facilitated through Ignorance, Idleness and Isolation, elements of the environment surrounding the neglected child.

Because our rented home was so small and transparent of sound, I often overheard many episodes of what went on in our family that kids were not supposed to hear. One such episode which is branded in my memory's store was my Mom threatening one of my male cousins who had exposed himself to my brother and me. On a day when Mom was at work, another woman to whose care we had been entrusted left us alone to be with her boyfriend. My 19-year-old cousin came into our home drunk and challenged our upbringing. There was a noise on the front porch at that very moment, interrupting his exposing himself and advancing suggestions to us. We, at five and four years of age, were crying because he threatened to "beat us up" if we told anyone. When our baby sitter returned, she was startled to see him and asked him what he was doing in the house. She yelled at us for letting him in and asked him to leave in a voice loud enough to attract one of our neighbors, Mr. Foyer, the barber. He came up on the porch and yelled, "Is everything all right in there?"

My cousin, a man of 6' 2" stature and twenty years of conditioned physical maturity, stumbled out the door and past Mr. Foyer. "What are you doing in Mrs. Naulls' house? You know no one is allowed in the house except the lady who takes care of her kids when she's at work!" He swore at Mr. Foyer, calling him names that my brother and I knew to be bad words. He made a prideful gesture at Mr. Foyer but suddenly his facial expression went from macho confidence to horrified retreat as Mr. Foyer pulled a pistol from his pocket and said, "What did you call me, boy?" My cousin ran back into the house and tried to get behind the babysitter and us but we all began crying and fled toward the security beneath the bed. Again, "What did you call me, boy?" yelled Mr. Foyer from deep within his indignation. "I'll blow your head off your no-good-sorry butt."

"I'm sorry, Mr. Foyer," came the responding cry. "I'm drunk and I don't know what I'm doing. I'll never say anything like that again." By this time, Mr. Foyer was standing astride my cousin's cowering down folded up body in the corner of the room in plain view of our horrified eyes. Mr. Foyer screamed, "I'm almost killing you, boy, and I don't know if I can stop myself. You no good sorry excuse for a man. You talked about me like I was a dog and I don't like that, boy!" Mr. Foyer's trembling and shaking ebbed into a deep sign and he released, "Get on out of here, boy, and don't ever come around here no more!" As my cousin crawled, then ran out the door, Mr. Foyer said to us, "You boys all right? Did he hurt you? Did he touch you, young lady?" We all shook our heads and said no in unison and Mr. Foyer assured us that "he wouldn't bother us no more."

When my mother crossed the color divide of living quarters into our neighborhood, she was informed of what the grapevine had developed about the day's events at her home. Running the ten or so blocks to our house, she arrived with a burst through the door, panting, "Where are my babies? Billy and William, where are you?" We rushed out of the back bedroom into her outstretched arms. She cried and held us and listened patiently to hear everything we had to say about what she never told us that she knew a version of already. Later on that evening we settled in with a reassurance that every-thing would be just fine now that Mama was home. She would deal with any and everybody who would dare to invade her home.

I never thought about it until later, but my father was never there, **Vanguarding** as teacher, protector, guide and role model! My Mother was the VANGUARD of my life and she walked it, talked it and lived it by example and final result.

I overheard later – one evening through the wall – a whisper – that my cousin's throat had been cut *"from ear to ear."* In a tavern one night soon after Mom's famous lecture to him, a woman attacked him by surprise from the rear. No one ever identi-fied the murderer but my cousin left this life know-ing from my mother that he dare not come near us again. Mr. Foyer and my mother met and he pro-foundly apologized for putting us in harm's way by pistol *protecting us from harm's way.* My mother was speechless but thankful for Mr. Foyer's less than enviable position of being a savior/vigilante and, at the same time, an out-of-control, grounded in pride, gun-pointing endangerer of her children's welfare. From through the walls again, I heard from the lips of my aunt that Mr. Foyer and Mom cried together when she forgave him for the mess he had gotten himself into when he tried to help her boys. She never took us to his barber shop again. I never saw that babysitter again either.

The **Lesson** above may appear to be convoluted, but a closer analysis reveals the thread of positive influence to train up parents and children in the Way they should react to the world. My brother and I knew to tell my Mom everything. As we grew and matured, we saw time and time again that her solutions were always to our benefit. Children need parents' tough love – parents who, no matter what the pressure might be, make decisions that adhere to God's Standard of expected behavior. Mom's one-liners were like a spiritual lightning rod to the soul, encouraging each of my thoughts to do it God's Way. I hear her voice occasionally even now, encouraging my thoughts and words toward actions in righteousness.

"*Dare You Dream . . . ?*"

Dare you dream for a Mom so dear
whom the angels in heaven joyously cheer
when God's **Promise** is expressed so true
that through her faith does accrue
Hope in the world, as shining stars to glow
in search of a vessel, implanted to know
the maturity in blessings lost souls to share
Jesus' empathy and Love, her cross to bear

Eternity life's **Promise**, Mom's alive with the
    Lord
The Godhead and Their angels are on One
    accord
that through righteous living, there's victory
    every day
even through your faith, Christ's life did pay
Belief so strong, Covenant's Seed does grow,
reaping God's **Promise** through our Lord did
    sow

So, dare you dream for a Mom so dear
that God our Father makes it abundantly clear
that she's the image of **His perfect PLAN**
entrusted with His posterity, of Redemption's
    MAN

Lesson on the Base in Race

On a sultry summer evening the lightning bugs waltzed in a display of their individual purpose. From the front porch of my aunt's south Dallas home, a group of mothers watched as we kids were playing hide-and-seek from the base of a giant pecan tree in the shadows beyond the street light's reach. Amid the occasional burst of laughter and continuous chatter of this group of discerning church-going ladies congregated there were my mother, three of her sisters and a bonded group of neighboring women. Loud and clear I heard one declare immediately before an outburst, "A man ain't nothing but a dog."

Later that night, as Mom tightly tucked her four children into bed, I asked her, "What does it mean, that 'a man ain't nothing but a *dog*'? Will I grow up to be a *dog* when I'm a man, mama?"

She replied, "The lady who made that remark was abandoned by her husband and left with two little children to care for. So she is real hurt and might have been speaking out of that hurt. You will never be thought of as a dog *if* you do and say what God wants you to do and say. People say things that have nothing to do with God and the truth about who you are. Some people say colored women folk are smarter than colored men folk; others say all men are bad and all women are good and regardless of skin color all men are dogs. William, you must not listen to anybody – Black or White – who tells you that you are superior or inferior to anyone because you are a male or because of your skin color."

Lesson: God doesn't look at people as men do. God "looks on the heart" (I Samuel 16:7).

I swallowed that meal of the gospel according to Bettie Arlene Naulls, gulping, "Yes, Mama."

"Go to sleep now, William. Let's pray to God for guidance and strength, for you to be a good boy who grows up to be a man that no one thinks of as a dog because of what you do."

Be Who You Is

Imitation of Life
shallow image to be
someone else's production
false witness of the
worth that one comes with
tumbling down life's canal
'twas already in there
DNA's **TRUTH** to tell
uniqueness that God gives
at creation to compel

The Potter's message of expression,
His Way, His Life, to excel
Be who you are in Him
let your life's story sell
and do so with no fear
through actions consistent and bold
Let your witness from the rooftop
stop satan's messengers cold
Be who you is, a saint
because if you ain't who you is
you is who you ain't

Be a saint
and not an ain't
Pay attention to the saint, and not
    the ain't
Because you are
who God says you are
and not who the devil wants
you to imitate as you admire
him in the lifestyle and
behavior of those of his kingdom
here on earth!

Mom's responses to my questions were timely **Lessons** that fueled the direction of my soul's growth. Her soul food helped me to grow past thinking of myself in terms of people's stereotypes. The notion that I was more than a color designation forced me to think,

If not a Negro
or colored
or one of the other stereotypic categories
evil folk contrive,
who am I?

Of course, it took a lifetime of introspective meditation to meaningfully analyze this perspective. The world was busy intruding its values on whom it wanted me to remain in its perverted view – an adjective, and not a NOUN.

Mom's Lessons

William:

Obedience to God is required
Judgment by skin color is not of Him inspired
Know right from wrong – and just do it
Do good and not evil; be strong – pursue it
Your actions are no better than anyone can see
and nobody is better than you can be
so don't let what's around to see
entice you to become whom God didn't create
    you to be
Use your mind to stand against wrong's woo-
    ing
Think before you act in unwise doing
Don't be ashamed to say, "I don't know"
Wisdom is summoned when your mind wants
    to grow
Tell me when evil does approach
to violate my teaching, your soul to broach
going beyond the boundary of appropriate
    action
to violate your person for their satisfaction
Care for yourself and your personal hygiene
live by the Standard of our Lord Supreme
Study in school; observe the Word of Faith's
    test
Compete with yourself alone to be God's Best

The most destructive forces against young minds, in any community, are ignorance and idleness, where nothing constructive to learn from those who are in a position to teach is offered. Often the teachers and role models of my socially and economically deprived section of Dallas were older boys and relatives.

On a muggy summer day in the alleyway between 10th and 9th Streets, my cousin Paul Wayne oozed confidence as he forced a fight between a mongrel dog and a homeless cat. He was six years or so older than all of us who watched him through five-year-old awed lenses. In the fierce battle that ensued, the cornered and retreating cat somehow attached itself to the underbelly of the dog, with its claws dug deeply into both sides and its teeth lodged into the space between the dog's front legs and the beginning of its throat. The dog was stunned and clearly did not know what to do with the position his physically inferior victim had taken. The mongrel mix of Shepherd and Boxer looked puzzled, whining, his eyes begging anybody for assistance. Paul Wayne, the dog's master, fearlessly walked over, grabbed the dog's head with one hand and tore the cat's paws loose with the other. The cat scampered away quickly as the dog nervously staggered sideways, barking a non-pursuing growl of relief, stumbling in the opposite direction from the cat's escape, to a corner of the alley, to sit, lick his wounds and regroup.

That event reminds me of the attitudes and vantage points in the relationship between Blacks and Whites in the South during my youth. The cat wasn't looking for a fight but found itself in a staged event out of its control, fighting in its boss's arena for its life. In my birthplace's environment, Black skinned people, in survival mode, attached them-selves to the underbellies and throats of White skinned people. **The Master**, who created all skin colors to live in the freedom of choice, was the only ONE who could loose the grip of the claws from the belly and the teeth from the throat of *him* who was inspired and trained by Paul Wayne to participate in this *cock fight* competition. The trainer's ultimate goal was assassination of his prey through another. The perceived power of White skin over Black skin was merely a temporarily imposed will until such time as the teeth of the *cat* reached the jugular of the *dog's* neck. Life's justice is imputed when the **Master** intervenes, supernaturally, to offer both hunter and prey a solution and *salvation* for both.

Did my cousin Paul Wayne realize that he mirrored the devil's attempt to contrive conflict between identifiable categories of God's creatures, "to kill, steal and destroy" all life? I'm sure he didn't, as he ventured to amuse himself and all of us, his pupils, wandering in that *alley of ignorance and idleness*. The fear of exploitation and death, the theft of freedom and the destruction of family purpose: This was the agenda of those who used these tactics to dominate us cats who walked upright on two legs. The dog's domination over the cat was neutralized when the cat fought its way into a different position. The two were stuck in an untenable *stalemate* – until the Master stepped in and loosed them. Only **the King** has a move at that point, in the stalemate of life's drama. He is the only possible solution. The **Truth** is that justice is that final bell to ring through freedom – to sing – **"By grace is salvation for all through faith in the King."**

Say It Loud, Mama,
IN Your Responsibility

I thank you, Jesus, for another day,
A consistent Word that my Mom did pray
Over our lives, about the dogs she was clear –
beware of them all –
but those with two legs to especially fear.
They'll put it in the food
and in the doctrines you drink,
complacency's mood, teaching you not to
    think
and from their messengers, what you're given
    to hear
they'll brainwash your mind, your conscience
    to sear.

She said, "Grab this Vine, of God's Life
    bearing Tree,
Precious Hope for your future that He gave
    to me.
Don't let go, hook it up to the core of your
    heart,
no matter what they say, hang on to what
    God gave you to start
your life's journey, when I'm not there to be
a Vanguard and protector, He'll remind you
    as He does me."

So I have benefited from the Faith
Mama voiced into me,
positive words of encouragement produced
    my fruit bearing tree.
Depending on watering for life's prosperity
God's bound to the increase
of the industry Mom's **Lessons** aroused in me.

I lived the gut-wrenching racial integration and transformation of collegiate and professional sports in America. I experienced first hand the power of talent's influence to merit inclusion into these institutions separated by Color. Influenced by **Pride to Win It All** and the **Love of Money**, the White folk lured the Black folk into the World of Entertainment Supply and Demand. All of us are the product of that pregnancy. The time has come for every voice to be tried by our ears alone.

My journey from underneath the belly of that dog called racism has been a lessening of my death grip into the color of an imposing hide, to the pressing on "to take hold of that for which Christ Jesus took hold of me" (Philippians 3:12b). Were there any lasting effects of that vantage point – hanging on, with my teeth and claws embedded, riding underneath that satanically directed dog? Who had the advantage then and what benefit has my fought-for freedom afforded me?

Lesson: My body is free, to allow my soul to be whoever God's given me. Acculturation inside, integration to ride, in Christ's Peace to hide. Black Folk and White Folk, skin deep in the *hide*, looking for a solution for the hate of the other to subside. We've got to overcome the confusion caused by Paul Wayne's *tempter's* delusion – for he contrived the intrusion of a *free ride*.

Grandmother Georgia Silver Naulls

*Grandma and Grandpa, reduced to print
never saw either during their stint
not even a photo of him did survive
but all of his offspring, nineteen in number, did arrive
I was robbed of heritage
by that dog called racism – to persist
until God gave, through the faith of His Son, in us to resist!*

Black Folks & White Folks

Black Folks and White Folks, like Rhythm
    and Blues,
historically wed partners now paying some
    dues

Blacks brought here to feed, Whites bought
    into the greed
but both came together wrought of satanic
    seed

Sown into their psyche satan's roots did
    drive
his message of anxiety and fear for each
    partner to derive

Oppressed and Oppressor, living hide by
    side
bound in "the love of money" and the habit
    of a free ride
Two hundred and four score plus of years
    did color impose its fervor
as water seeking its shallow ground did
    base in them endeavor

As fuel in the rage of hatred of a forced will
    upon the other
two races made stronger yet through
    reproductive – but – abused Black
    Mother

Struggling in extreme identity, wanting to
    stop the flow
of erupting melting oneness, genetic colors
    did grow

Like a dual-headed monster, DNA giving
    God's woman to share
color's panic of survival, racism's motives
    are hers to bear

God has said, only in MY SON can one
    know how to survive
the devil's schemes to kill all skin colors
    through the plot he did contrive

So – Black Folks and White Folks, like
    Rhythm and Blues,
join in syncopated harmony, let empathy for
    weakness peruse

Knowing how tangled the web was spun,
how hatred of skin color was wickedly
    begun
try glorifying God in this lifetime to see
people loving one another in Christ Jesus'
    decree

Summer Vacation without my Mother

with My Dad, Brother and Uncle's Charm Meeting My Relatives Down on their Sharecropping Farm

At the beginning of the summer of my fifth year of life outside the womb, my father convinced my mother to let him take his two older boys on vacation with him to meet their relatives. Most of his family lived in east Texas near the Arkansas border. My brother and I eagerly awaited him on the morning of our departure and were doubly excited to learn that our favorite Uncle Million was going on the trip with us. He was so much fun to be around and always had something in his right pocket as a surprise for us. This time it was *red hots*, the little red bits of candy with something hot inside. We loved them because they were sweet and chewy and exploded within our taste buds.

As we drove through the streets of Dallas and passed areas I had never seen before, I noticed the stark contrast between the streets' pavement and width, the stores, cars and dress and *color of the skin* of the people from that of the area we lived in. As a child I thought nothing about socioeconomic injustices because no men around spoke the underlying truth before me. They rarely spoke of the racist attitudes of Whites toward Blacks or of hope for a better day before their kids. We rode in an eerie silence and were well out of the city limits before my uncle relieved the tension and began to entertain us with jokes and stories about people he

Billy and William with Father Daily

Dallas, Texas

from a photograph
original painting by Martin Payton

The sun was bright
we grimaced from its light
as the camera recorded the rarity
 of this scene
with my dad and my brother
we're so close to each other
as only would happen in my dream

knew and places he'd been.

At the first gas station where we stopped to refuel, I saw signs that I did not understand: "For Whites Only." My father told me to "hold it a bit longer" when I asked him about going to the bathroom. "As soon as we get back on the open highway, we can stop by the road so you can tinkle." I also saw my father's submissive attitude toward the young White men who filled the tank with gas and glared past all of us as though we didn't exist. My father called them "sir" and said "Yes, sir" as he bowed his head and dipped his knees in obedient submission of his manhood. My brother and I were being trained up in the way of Black skin male survival in the south.

The trip was long and hot, even with all the windows down. We finally turned off the main highway into a wooded area outside Marshall, Texas, drove for a few miles, then took a left turn up a slight incline into an area in front of an old run-down house. Dad blew his horn and six or seven children ran out of the house to greet us. They ranged in age from barely walking to their early teens. Following them out the door was a tall, handsome man who looked very much like my dad and uncle – and a beautiful olive brown skinned woman. This was Dad's family –Uncle Lyke and his wife, Aunt Mayelu. My dad said, "Sons, this is your uncle and auntie, and all of these kids are your first cousins!" The kids surrounded my brother and me and we were off to play without hesitation. A while later, out of the corner of my eye I saw my dad and uncle driving away, down the road. My immediate reaction was fear and panic. Tears were on their way when my cousins grabbed me and we were off and running again. The excitement of being the center of attention of all these new relatives who liked me covered my tears with joy.

The sun was on its way toward the end of another day before I realized that this was the beginning of my first night away from Mom. Through the distraction of all these relatives of mine, I had forgotten to miss her. As I lay on the floor among several other kids who slept there routinely, I gazed up through the nail holes in the tin covering the ceiling and could see clear through to the stars. I asked one of my cousins, "How do you keep the rain from coming in here?" He said, "You don't." I was too tired to entertain the thought of fear. The next sound which awakened me was a rooster crowing. It was morning already. As the light from the sun's rays formed its own pattern through the holes in the tin roof against the back-drop of the sparsely furnished room and white-washed walls, I opened my eyes to experience the beginning of our first full day on the farm. This was to be a summer in which I would learn volumes of life maturing **Lessons**.

I was all smiles after gorging myself on all the biscuits and eggs and bacon and butter and molasses and milk that I wanted. After I finished eating breakfast with my newly discovered relatives, including Dad's half-brother Uncle Gideon (Gid) and half-sister Aunt Cora, we were told that it was time to go to work. I got very excited about *picking cotton* because adults in Dallas had glorified *"the best pickers they had ever seen"* in stories young folk heard from as long as I could remember. We walked out into the early morning east Texas sun and down the road "a piece" to the cotton fields. The cotton was higher than I was and the sack to put the cotton in was as long as – well – any sack I had ever seen.

By noon I had tried every tactic known to me to get out of the hot sun. It turned out that working to pick those long unending rows of cotton was not very much fun after all. I determined that I didn't want to be in the Hall of Fame of Cotton Pickers. The first **Lesson** I learned away from Mom was that crying didn't change anything. The second **Lesson** was that continuing to cry and whine was not tolerated. My aunt was twice the size of my mother and she was no-nonsense. There wasn't any need for physical punishment because just the mention of telling my father altered my attitude. The sun bore brighter and brighter into my skin and I learned that the purpose of the sharecropping farming Naulls family was to "pick," not "pull," these acres of cotton as partial payment for living on the White man's land.

At noontime, our family members came together and sat down in a grove of peach trees. Our lunches were stored in large recycled lard and molasses cans. The food was the best I had ever tasted: fried chicken on top of biscuits on top of greens and beans. For dessert I pulled a peach which was reddish green – or maybe greenish red. Later that day I knew why my aunt had cautioned me not to eat the fruit, as she had said, "It's not ripe, William, and not good for you. It will make you sick." I did eat the *forbidden fruit* and it took days before my stomach settled enough for the food I ate to benefit my body. My aunt taught me a **Lesson** in grace as she consoled me in my groaning.

After leaving Uncle Lyke's farm, my father took

us to meet Aunt Easter and Uncle Buster on their farm in Domino, Texas. Aunt Easter, the eldest of Dad's sisters and brothers, was very tall and Uncle Buster was much much shorter than she, standing about 5' 8" tall. They too had cotton to be picked and peas to "shed" and corn to "cut." These relatives of mine were always busy, it seemed to me, and after a while I loved every minute of it. They never went to the store except to buy flour, sugar and salt, etc. When they wanted to have meat with a meal, either they killed a cow, a hog or a chicken or they shot a rabbit, a squirrel or a pheasant or they fished the water holes in the area. The corn, tomatoes, beans and fruit were preserved along with the nuts for pies. Everything grown was harvested and either consumed or canned for use during the winter months. *What a great life*, I thought. And huge watermelons. The size Mom bought in the store in Dallas they fed to the hogs and chickens. We ate the best of the best – and all we could eat. My muscles grew, and my height and confidence as well. *What a great life. It can't get any better!*

Aunt Easter's only child was Cousin Felix McGilvery. He and his wife, Cousin Dessie, had four children: Cousins Dessie, Dorothy, Raye and M.H. (Million Harvest McGilvery, or Mac, who would, years later in California, be San Pedro High School's first All-City basketball player). Their house was smaller and we only slept there one night. They had a mule and Cousin Felix let me hold the reins to guide him as he plowed his fields. "Git-te up, Mule. Whoa, Mule. Gee, Mule. Haw, Mule." He let me say the commands. *If my friends in Dallas could see me now*, I thought. The family horse was called Ol' Blue Blade. He was reputed to be the fastest horse in that area. Ol' Blue was kind of short with a reddish coat and a long, long tail. I begged Cousin Felix to let me ride the horse. Riding horses looked real simple to me. I saw the cowboys racing across the screen in the movies and I was sure that if they could do it, I could too. I would just kick him in the sides, pull on the reins, lean forward and shout, "Hi Yo, Blue Blade," and away we would go.

Cousin Felix finally acquiesced to my plea after I promised him that I wouldn't kick the horse in the sides and that I would hold the reins tightly to control him. "He's real sensitive, William, so just go slowly and you won't get him excited," Cousin Mac and Uncle Buster warned me. At the point when they helped me up on Ol' Blue Blade, we were about half way from Cousin Felix's house en route to Aunt Easter's. I was so excited. The only thing that held me back was Uncle Buster's gaze into my eyes. "William, look at me! You mind us, do you hear? This horse can be dangerous and he's real fast." I assured Uncle Buster that I wouldn't do anything wrong. He finally gave me the reins and I had the power of a horse at my command. I didn't understand at the time that power would corrupt me absolutely, causing me to lose all reason, with the potential of losing my life.

I had visions of being the Lone Ranger on Silver followed by Tonto on Scout, pursuing outlaws as in movies and on the radio. I leaned forward and pulled the reins tight and kicked Ol' Blue Blade in his sides as hard as I could. He lunged forward and we were off. As I passed several people, mostly my relatives on the side of the road, they were all yelling at me with desperate expressions on their faces.

"Pull up on the reins, William!" I ignored them, punched Ol' Blue Blade again in his sides with my heels and screamed, "Let's go, Big Blue!" We were one with the wind as we raced through a field and across an area beside the barn where clothes were hung out to dry. I didn't see the clothes line, but I did see Ol' Blue Blade continuing toward the barnyard without me. A line caught my neck and upper body and sling-shot me up in the air like an out of control amateur trapeze performer.

On my way down to earth I saw Aunt Easter's concerned face covered partially by her hands. My tail bone hit the ground first with such force that I didn't feel the trauma of the rest of my body bouncing around like an under-inflated basketball. I lay still for a moment, then tried to catch my breath to roll over but couldn't. I thought every chicken, cow, pig, dog and relative of mine had their eyes and attention focused on me and were barely able to control their laughter. What a fool I had made of myself. I slowly rolled over on my side and began to get up. My tail bone hurt more than my pride so I began to cry. I thought of *Mama* but I was glad she wasn't there. Her **Lesson** rang in my mind: "A hard head leads to a soft behind." My punishment was not a paddle, but a *fall* on my butt.

Later on that day, just prior to dinner, I heard the men laughing about the special horse show Ol' Blue Blade and I had put on for them. No one chastised me and only Uncle Buster voiced everyone's concern as he passed me moaning on the ground, "You all right, William?" "Yes, sir," I answered! A few days passed before the soreness wore off and my mind cleared enough to think back to my ride on Ol' Blue Blade. They wouldn't let me

near him after my disobedient action, which was
punishment severe because I surely wanted to ride
him again and befriend the first horse I had ever
been introduced to.

On our way back to Dallas after two months, we
stopped to visit Uncle Zero who had eleven kids.
They didn't have any place for us to sleep but it was
really fun meeting more of my mounting number of
cousins. There were Cousins James and Wilbur and
Billy and Ray and the other seven. Wow! The
Naulls men and their male children sure looked
alike. We kids played and ran until it was time to
leave the farm. Uncle Zero's face flashed before me
recently. He and his sons James and Wilbur, when
they were grown up, were Clark Gable look-alikes,
in Technicolor, of course.

As we drove toward Dallas, a huge trailer truck
transporting merchandise tried to run my dad off
the road into a ditch. In one of the few times that I
heard him contemplating out loud, he asked my
uncle why he thought White folk hated Black folk
so much that they were willing to try to kill entire
families just because they *wanted* to and *could get
away with it*. My uncle's response was thought
provoking and encouraging. He said, "Ah, Dale, it's
better than it used to be and not as good as it's going
to get. Everything is getting better as time passes
every day. White people can't spend all their time
and their lives hating Black people. That's a full
time job and a waste of their lives. They'll leave us
alone some day when they get tired of holding us
back and find something more productive to do
with their time. The boys here will not have to go
through what we've been through."

In what seemed to be no time at all, we were

greeted at the front door of our home by Mom's smiling face. I thought I saw a trace of a tear of joy in her eyes as she hugged us and escorted us inside. Soon Dad was gone with Uncle Million and I was in a big tub of warm sudsy water. It was comforting to have Mom washing behind my ears and neck and to feel her presence as she tucked us into bed with a loving good night kiss. It took weeks to tell her about all the things we learned and did on the farm. I did notice the peace and quiet away from the sounds of mooing and barking and clucking and oinking and git-te-up-mule – and the pre-dawn rooster's wake up call. Yes, it was good to be back home, but I'll never forget my first summer away from Mom. Interesting to note: Mom did her job so well that each of her children remembers the special attention she paid to each one of us. That's Hall of Fame parenting. Her motive was always to do the will of God through serving her children, her family and her community.

My First Job

Looking forward to my first real job was the most exciting anticipation I had ever known. I was so anxious to do some meaningful work, to be of service to people who would pay me money for doing something to their benefit. Do you remember your first job? Do you remember the awesome feeling of accomplishment and worth when the boss gave you your first wages? Wow! What a sense of being responsible, of being independent, or at least of being on your way toward independence. I take you back to our home on Bettington Circle in the Oak Cliff section of Dallas. I don't remember my dad being around very much; but when I was old enough to ask, I knew that he had made the decision that I wasn't his priority.

Mr. Trimble, the ice man, was my first boss. Of course, Dad and Mom were my real bosses, but you know what I mean. The first person to whom my parents delegated their authority was Mr. Trimble, the ice man. Back in those days people had no refrigerators but had ice boxes to keep things cold and food from spoiling. Mr. Trimble used a truck to deliver ice to our neighborhood and we were one of the customers on his route. I'll never forget the day he asked my mother, after placing a fifty-pound block of ice into our ice box, "How old's that boy, Mrs. Kid?" (That's what everyone called my mom, "Mrs. Kid.")

She replied, "He's seven years old, Mr. Trimble."

"Sho' is a big un, Mrs. Kid. That boy is big enough to get a job! Do you want to work for me, boy?" Before I knew what had happened, Mr. Trimble told my mother, who had left the decision up to me, that I was his assistant. I assured him that I could carry a 25 pound block of ice on my back!! Yeah! And all day long if necessary!

The next day at 6:00 a.m., there was a knock at our door and I stepped out onto the porch ready to carry me some ice to somebody's ice box. I did not care whose, but I knew I could live up to Mom's expectation that I would do my best. *Yeah!* I thought to myself, *I will carry these 25 pound blocks of ice on my back into the homes of these neighbors of ours, and I will not embarrass my family. If necessary, I know I can carry a 50 pound block! Yeah!* As I followed Mr. Trimble off our front porch, I noticed for the first time that he descended the three steps with great difficulty, in obvious pain. One of his legs was clearly much longer than the other and was crooked inward at the knee joint. As I stepped up on the running board of the truck, Mr. Trimble snapped, "Git on in the truck, boy; I ain't got all day."

"Yes, sir," was my reply, as I remembered my mom's words to Mr. Trimble, "If my boy gives you any trouble, you let me know, Mr. Trimble."

"Yes, ma'am, Mrs. Naulls," was his reply. "I sho' 'nuff will!" His eyes glanced a threatening punishment toward me if I dared to challenge his authority or act disrespectfully toward him.

En route in that old Model A or T truck to the ice house to pick up our first load of ice, a feeling of entrapment began to seep into my consciousness. My mind drifted to wonder where my friends were and what they would be doing during this hot summer Dallas day. "What time do we finish today,

Mr. Trimble?" I asked.

He snapped back, his voice cracking like Zorro's whip, "You ain't picked up one block of ice yet, boy, and you already thinking about going to play. Do you want to work, boy?"

"Yes, sir," I said, hoping that he wasn't already disappointed in me. I sure hoped he wouldn't tell my mom I had asked that stupid question.

As the day progressed, I became accustomed to the leather covering for carrying ice on my right shoulder. I liked picking the ice up with the ice hooks, putting the block up on my back with Mr. Trimble's help, and treading up the walkway of each house, in through the front door, across the living/dining room, and into the kitchen. I then eased the ice off my shoulder onto the kitchen floor, readjusted my hooks, picked the ice back up and gently dropped it into the open space in the top of the ice box. After closing the top, I tipped my head and thanked the people for doing business with Mr. Trimble.   By lunch time I was so hungry that thoughts of opening Mr. Trimble's big lunch box danced through my head. Finally he said, "It's time to eat," and I reached for his box, forgetting that Mom had made me a lunch. He simply said, "Boy," as he pointed to my lunch bag, "that's yours and this is mine!"

"Yes sir, Mr. Trimble; sorry, Mr. Trimble," was all I could say. After saying a brief prayer, I ate my sandwich so fast that I again reached for Mr. Trimble's box with my eyes. His eyes won the battle and when I realized that I still had more hours of work, my stomach voiced its demand for more food.

When he finally let me out of the truck around 2:00 p.m., I ran into my mother's arms as she waited for me, looking through our front screen door. I smiled and gave her my first day's wages, a nickel. She was so proud of me and told me to tell her everything that had happened. As I finished my exhaustingly long, blow-by-blow story, she smiled as she hung on to my every word. I was so thankful for the wonderful experience Mr. Trimble had opened up to me.

Sometime during the third week of my six-day-a week job, Mr. Trimble thought I had handled the 25 pound block of ice on my back sufficiently well, so he said, "Boy, can you carry 50 pounds of ice?"

"Uh . . . yes, sir . . . Mr. Trimble."

He said, "You sure, boy?"

This time his voice challenged me and I let him know that, *yeah*, correcting my voice to a *yeah, I can handle that any day* tone. "Yes, sir, Mr. Trimble, I can carry 50 pounds of ice." A few stops later, after I had reassured him of my confidence, he helped me put a block of – whatever it was – on my back. It felt like a heaviness I had never experienced, maybe a Mack truck on my back. I don't know, but it was the most difficult of decisions to continue on this trip my ego had overloaded my back with. My teeth and lips ground a foolish determination as Mr. Trimble's strong hands steadied me. Then I reeled off one step to the right, then back two.

He grabbed me, shouting, "Boy, can you carry 50 pounds of ice?"

I grunted, "Uh-huh, yes, sir, Mr. Trim . . . ble!" He then let go, pushing me in the direction of the house. I stepped up on the first step, then the second, and finally I lunged toward the front door, using its frame to stop my momentum.

Fortunately the lady of the house saw my

struggle and opened the door. I let go of the door jamb, freeing my shoulder to balance my next two steps toward the kitchen. What came to mind when I found myself stumbling in the middle of the room was panic. I leaned toward the kitchen, taking shorter and faster steps as my knees buckled. Finally, my body swung a sharp thrust to the right, and with a rolling motion, I released the 50 pound block onto the linoleum floor. The ice sped across the floor like a bowling ball, wiping out a big black metal wood-burning heater next to the wall. Bellows of black soot shot up into the air as debris from the table and some shelves scattered all over the room. As I looked up in fear at the lady of the house, she had a contorted expression on her face of wait-'til-I-get-my-hands-on-you. In her eyes I saw doom for myself. As she started toward me I was already on my way out the door. When my feet left the porch in a pivot to the left, I was just out of the reach of Mr. Trimble's out-stretched hands. I quickly distanced myself from him in the opposite direction, hearing his voice yelling, "Boy, what have you done?"

The lady was screaming at me, and then she turned on Mr. Trimble, shouting, "Why did you let that young boy bring that big thing of ice by himself? My house is ruined." Mr. Trimble was at a loss for words. I looked back over my shoulder from a block or so away and could see Mr. Trimble entering the house with the lady, probably to help her clean up the mess and survey the damage my ego had done. What a fix I had gotten myself into.

When I finally got home, I told my Mom what had happened and that I had run almost all of the many blocks home. She put my face between her hands and said, "Are you all right, honey? You did your best and that's all anyone can expect of you. You wanted to work, so I let you, and maybe now we know that you are too young for that kind of work."

I said, "What about Mr. Trimble? He's mad at me, real mad."

"I'll take care of Mr. Trimble, honey. He won't be mad at you. He knows that 50 pounds of ice is too much for you. So don't worry."

I said, "Thank you, Mama," and rested my head on her lap. *What a relief,* I thought, *to have Mama to straighten out all the mistakes I make.*

I never saw Mr. Trimble again – face to face, that is. I did see his truck from time to time, and I saw other older assistants on his truck with him; but I always ran in the opposite direction, when *"the ice man cometh."* I even ran and hid at night when he occasionally limped, with a growl and a scowl on his face, into my dreams. But what a **Lesson** I learned about working and getting paid for it. I enjoyed it so much, I've been working in that seed planting of a work ethic ever since. Mr. Trimble represented the world testing my mind and leaving the decision up to me whether or not I was old enough and physically strong enough to "carry the ice." Mom, God bless her, stood over my environmental experience, but allowed and encouraged, even demanded of me, that I do things and learn things for myself.

Lesson: "Doing things for yourself and working out your own maturation, William, facilitates your growth in dignity." I can hear my mother's words toning me down when another voice outside of me tried to negatively control my thoughts: **"Don't let your mouth overload your butt, William. Let people be surprised by what you can do, and that's a lot."**

The transition, from growing strong through being allowed to do things for myself under the watchful eye of a Godly parent, to teaching that principle of growth to my children and others, is a giant challenge of the serious kind. My first job experience was a foundational step in developing into the man God had created me to be. There is no substitute for hard work and challenges for our minds and bodies. The choices we make and what we do in the midst of those challenges mold our character.

"Voices"

In the silence, of where I do hear
above the noises, where my thoughts are
    formed clear
come suggestions from two different **voices**
urgently appealing to counsel my **choices**

The decision is mine about which **voice** to
    trust
Even the unlearned knows that
    information's a must
To make a **choice** that benefits my position
requires obeying the **Voice** that yields
    Godly fruition

Faith to choose a direction is a determina-
    tion to walk
stepping out into the deep waters of which
    the **voices** talk
Now, there's this **voice** who cunningly
    imposes that wrong is right
But the **One Voice** who saved me says,
    "**Stand** . . . " in the good faith fight

The **One Voice** promises, "I'll never forsake
    you or leave you flat."
The other **voice** counters, "Did the **One
    Voice** who promised really say that?"
The other **voice** continues, "Worship me to
    become as the Most High's Choice."
The **One Voice** says, "My sheep who love
    Me know and respond to My **Voice**."

The direction of one's life is compassed in
    choices,
couched in heart's recesses, influenced by
    voices
So, be careful what you hear, and know that
    blessed is your choice
when you act in **Faith**, in the **Good
    Shepherd's Voice**!

Lesson on Choice and Predestination:
Moving from Dallas to Los Angeles
Resurrected My Life's Choices

My Mother taught me the foundational **Lessons** of expected behavior before entrusting me to my first teacher, Miss Billie Montgomery. Miss Montgomery had a private school kindergarten which took a selective number of pupils each year. She was very stern and our parents gave her the absolute authority to discipline us if we were disrespectful or talked in class. Very prominent in the corner behind her desk, in plain view of each student, were her rods of correction, *switches*. Branches from trees stripped of their leaves stood tall, from floor to . . . reaching above our heads. Her one room class was the most disciplined, demanding and fulfilling of my school days. By the time that year of instruction had ended, I knew my times tables from 1 X 1 to 12 X 12 – and – *how to read*. I took second place in the year's final spelling bee to the shortest girl in the class. My Mom stated on many occasions that she was convinced that Miss Montgomery's one year with a child would have him or her prepared to a standard high enough to compete with *any* first grade student in the country.

Any notion of Miss Montgomery's educational environment continuing over into public school was shattered a few months later. My mother enrolled me in N. W. Harlee Public Grammar School, just a few blocks from Miss Montgomery's haven on 8th Street. On the first day of school, Mom dressed us in neatly pressed short pants and starched shirts with suspenders, white socks and shoes. The moment she let go of my hand and said, "Be a good boy in school – I love you," my brother left me on my own to find my way. Three older boys walked up to me and said, "Give me your lunch. You got any money?" Of course I refused and they attacked me, throwing dirt all over me and knocking me to the ground. I cried and went to the school office as Mom had instructed me to do and told the principal what had happened. He took me by the hand and walked me out on the playground and I pointed out the boys. He ordered them to meet him in his office and told them that fifth graders shouldn't pick on first graders. Later on that day, one of the boys walked by me and slapped me on the side of my head. He was upset because Mr. Pimpton, the principal, had given him and his friends three swats each on their behinds. I just stared at him. When I got home that afternoon, my mother asked me how my day went. I told her, "Not so good," and shared with her my bewilderment as to why these boys didn't like me and hit me. "Why, Mama?"

She said, "Some people don't think very much of themselves. They don't attack other boys or girls of their age because it would be more of a challenge than taking advantage of a *sweet child like* you." As I eased closer and deeper into her bosom, she said, "I don't want you fighting, William. Do you hear me? Christian folk let the Lord do their protecting and I'll go with you to school tomorrow and have a talk with those boys who attacked my baby. Now you get ready for bed and we'll pray to God for guidance."

The next morning as I stood halfway behind and close to her left leg in front of the school, Mom's presence gave me a serene security all over as the kids spoke politely to her. My finger pointed out the villains and before one of the boys knew what was upon him, my mother, in her firmness, asked what his name was. He told her. She then told him that she knew his mother and the fathers of three of them who had attacked her child. "Don't you ever hit my boy again – and I will be over to your house this evening to talk to your folks." The boy responded on the spot that he was very sorry and begged Mom not to tell his dad. The other two came over and apologized also, and the scene was over. I don't think Mom ever told their parents because between the swats of Mr. Pimpton with the paddle and the threat of more punishment from their parents before them, they never bothered me again.

Lesson: Mom trained her children up to "trust in the Lord. God will fight your battles." When I was older, even when I was intentionally wrong, I did not stray far from her teaching because I knew that I was wrong. I am convinced that a child has very little chance of developing into the full measure of his or her created purpose without the nurture and loving training of his or her Godly parent.

My 1st and 2nd grade teacher, whose name, I believe, was Miss Bailey taught me well in reading, writing and arithmetic. She approached me during class one day about my entering a school singing contest. Without thinking I said, "Yes, Ma'am, I will." I told my Mom and she told all of our relatives and friends. All of a sudden I experienced another kind of fear – the thought of making a fool out of myself in front of the entire school. When the date arrived, the audience was filled with kids and our parents. Then it happened! I was called to go up on the stage and sing. When I had settled in place, the music from the piano was loud and clear as rehearsed as it introduced the beginning of my song. I opened my mouth and an exhaling muted breath of *nothing* came out. Well, the kids let out a roar of laughter and pointed at me so loud and piercing that it took my breath away. Our teacher quickly came up on the stage and put her arm around me and asked if I were all right. I nodded my head up and down with my eyes wide open. She scolded the kids for their *"insensitivity and rudeness."* Then she asked me if I would please sing for everyone – but I could sit down if I chose to. I said, "OK, I'll sing." The song was introduced again and I completed my commitment to sing.

Someone else won the contest and as we were walking home, my mother had her arm around me and asked me how I felt when the kids were laughing at me. "Terrible, and I'll never do that again," I moaned. She said, "It's not good to make decisions about your future when things don't turn out the way you like the first time you try. You did just fine, William." Later on that night, just before closing my eyes, I heard this **Lesson: "It's not a good thing for you to let people's negative reaction to what you attempt discourage you. It took a lot of courage to get up there on that stage and I'm proud of you – real proud, especially that you finished what you started. Those that laughed at you may never experience what you did tonight. So, I'm real proud of you, William!"** I tightened my grip on her arm, sensing that she was allowing me to wade further from her shore into the deeper waters of my evolving independence. Where had she learned all those timely words? How did she know what to say in every situation? As I closed my eyes, she prayed to God for guidance and wisdom for both of us to embrace as food for our souls.

That *Guidance* word my mother talked about so casually, yet with such confidence in God, meant to me that God would direct me through any mine field in the darkest of nights. What a strong boost to my confidence I got when she tucked me into bed with a good night kiss, whispering, "Let's pray to God for Guidance." Everything was going to be all right in the morning. God Himself was working overnight on the enemy of our family. He fought our battles. Mom stressed to "just listen for God's Guidance," and He would be a lamp unto my feet and a light unto my path. The accuracy of God's Word demands adherence to its Truth, for there is *Guidance* therein.

Imagination that Wins

It takes one laugh
with her not in the flow
at whatever she's attempted to do
to derisively stunt her will to grow
One laugh – joined in by others –
shocks the soul where imagination resides
Her mind suspended – a long time to
    recover
mired in the RUT where insecurity abides
Imagination is so fragile in flight
as to inhabit thought in the still of the night
where laughter directed is an echo next door
absorbed in the carpet which covers that floor

Silence of slumber calls the soul to alert
the resources stored in one's heart – to exert
whatever her spirit wills to share with
    another
like the uniqueness of him, a daydreaming
    brother
Is it the mind who relaxes
for one's soul to reap –
what's deep within the abundance
that God gives one in sleep?
Or is it insecurities
caused by the opening bell's ringing
submitting your power to others
to judge one's talent in singing?
There's something real challenging
about standing up in front of folk
especially after experiencing
the ultimate brunt of their *joke*
Get up off the floor
and give it a try again
or you will miss the persistence
of exercising the power inside – to win!
Fear is thought a yellowing color
to be painted down every spine
which would turn and run
rather than in competition dine
Truth is – Free **Imagination that Wins**
embraces *God's Power* – and *Faith in Him* –
    twins

Both of my teachers through second grade were African American women, but that would soon change. By this time we had moved quite a few times in the Oak Cliff section of Dallas, from Bettington Circle to Judsten Court to Church Street – all on unpaved streets. There was an alley between Church Street and Eighth Street separating African American families and Anglo Americans. The White section began on the corner of Eighth and Fleming where Miss Montgomery's private home kindergarten school was located, behind the local candy store on the corner. The alley was the dividing line between Black skin folk and White skin folk. My Mother often told her children never to speak to nor look at a White man or woman. She didn't want us to be around people who openly "looked for ways to harm us and who didn't wish us well." On a day as I was coming home through the alley I noticed a boy my age standing near our back gate to the alley. We stopped, motionless, when we saw each other, standing only a few feet apart. He said, "Hi."

 "Hi," I replied.

"You want to play some marbles?" he asked, moving a little bit closer.

Before I could answer, a woman covered with White skin stormed out their back gate into the alley yelling his name. "You get back in this yard and don't you ever talk with that nigger boy again. You know better than that." He ran back through the gate into their backyard and the gate slammed behind him. I only saw him once or twice more, ever, but I often felt his presence peeking through the fence as I walked down the alley with the Randall boys. We shot marbles by their home on the corner of Fleming and the alley.

My mother heard of my encounter and she told me again, "William, don't go into that White boy's backyard or talk to him because his daddy and mama don't like our color. They and their friends don't mean us any good. Stay away from them, William, do you understand?"

"Yes, Mama, I understand."

Lesson: "Children, obey your parents in the Lord, for this is right. 'Honor your father and mother' – which is the first commandment with a promise – 'that it may go well with you and that you may enjoy long life on the earth.'" (Ephesians 6:1-3)

At an early age of consciousness, I found myself trapped in a body which inspired older boys to attack and inflict their pent-up frustrations and hostilities. I reasoned that genetics had played a mean trick on me and given me size superior to that of boys four to six years older. Once they found out that I was commanded by my parents not to fight back, they had no mercy on me. Daily they punched and kicked me and threw dirt on me just because I was big, healthy, washed and scrubbed, quiet and non-combative. Oh, how miserable those segregated years in that Dallas, Texas, ghetto were; Black hands bruising African Black bodies, in the name of evil's desire to dominate, violate, exploit and control.

The long range Southern White agenda of fear, intimidation and division was frustrated when God, in all His mercy, summoned my parents and their four children to Los Angeles, California. The profound impact on me was slow to evolve. After three days and three nights of sitting on boxes behind seats in a cramped, over-sold passenger car of the Southern Pacific Railroad train, in the colored-only section, we finally arrived at Union Station in downtown Los Angeles. My first impression was that L.A. was a slightly upgraded version of my Dallas home ghetto. The geographic location had changed, but the spirit of violence was the same.

At my new school, Ascot Avenue, I soon found that same loud expression and dislike of whom my parents were raising me to be: one who was slow to speak, quick to listen, and slow to get angry. New boys in the school had to fight their way to a place on the pecking order of one of the established *groups* on campus, and all of the boys made me the target of their confusion about who they were. As tension within me melted over into thoughts of using a baseball bat to eliminate the leaders of the most feared boys, my dad abruptly announced one evening that we were moving to San Pedro, California.

Yes, at nine years of age, I had enough fear stored up within my soul that the thought of violence to strike back at the source of my fear was mounting. The day I had planned to intentionally attack another human was the day after my father's announcement released the *pressure* of my *cooker*. I certainly never condoned violence, and I am confident that no one, not even my parents, nor the groups of intimidators, suspected that I was ready and looking for an opportunity to take some of those boys out. I had not been prepared by television or film examples of violence, because there were few movies depicting violence and no television in those days. Yet my instincts of self preservation of my human and civil rights raised up in me an attitude of

"I don't care what happens; I am going to stop them from invading my right to be left alone, to be me!"

Did You Ever Feel . . . . Did You?

Did you ever feel:
Wired in fear
with nothing to hold dear
any moment a tear
your future unclear

Did you ever feel you were in a:
Daily rut on track
with a lunch in a sack
off to school and back
constantly under attack?

Did you ever sense a need to:
Still your voice to survive
lest the violence to revive
pain and suffering yet alive
lest you still your soul to survive?

Did you ever just want to:
Be quiet and pass on by
those in your class – then a sigh
fear erupting in your eye
thinking they want you to die?

Did you ever joy when:
From the west Hope came
and He knew you by name
He and your Mom thought the same
inspiring you to get into life's game?

Did you ever smile when:
From the window of a train
you saw the earth in need of rain
near the ocean which collects the same
your fortune's vision for you to claim?

Did you ever cry:
When your mom had to die
knowing she's the reason why
your wings are strong enough to fly
and that the sparkle she put in your eye
has inspired people of all races to try
bearing fruit with the **SEED** to multiply?

Thank you, Mom!

Branded in my memory is the thirty-mile ride
from 43rd Place on the east side of Los Angeles to our
new home in the governmental housing projects of
San Pedro. Our destination and new address was
2530 Seaport Drive. Everything we owned was
packed in the back of a small flat bed truck with my
older brother, Bill, and me. There was an icy rain
which chilled us to the bone as we moved anxiously
south, down Central Avenue, then west on Slauson
Avenue, and a left turn south again toward the
shipyards of San Pedro via Avalon Boulevard.
Every so often Bill and I were comforted by our

mother's glance and empathic smile through the rear window of that truck. But – no peace was to be mine as I envied my younger twin brother and sister who were sleeping on Dad's and Mom's laps inside, where the living was easy and the cockpit was warm. When we finally arrived at the base of a hill in the dark of night, my lungs were filled with the fallout of the huge oil refinery which was in clear view just north of the little three-room house that I would live in for the next five years. We were all so happy just to be at our destination, finally, on the southeast side of a hill overlooking Todd Shipyard on the Pacific Ocean. The refinery's odor, which was thick all around us, was somehow ignored until another day.

Over the next few years, my new community became one in which I was allowed to emotionally breathe, to think unimpeded thoughts and to dare to communicate with people, without regard for color. People covered with White or Brown skin, people from Asia, Ireland, England, Mexico, Yugoslavia, Italy, the Philippines, and from the south, east, north and west in our country. Talk about a melting pot! We were it. The majority of us came to San Pedro in the name of supporting, repairing or preparing for action the war machine of the United States of America in our mission to stop German and Japanese aggression and their offensive plans to dominate the world and its resources.

MET-A-MOR-PHO-SIS

From worm-like to a butterfly
a choice given to each one to be worked out
Winged to soar in God's Purpose
Powered by Christ's Faith – in *no doubt*
Patiently awaiting within the Hope
in each developing young soul
is God's Promise at the end of the Rainbow
of Prosperity in each of His Pots of Gold
Metamorphosis to mankind is but a word
unless Christ is believed as the One
whom God has, in love, sent here
to get us back from where Adam did succumb

Recently, in October or November of 2003, I received a call from a man who said that in the mid-1940s his family was our neighbor in a housing project in San Pedro, California. His call shook my memory to recall his family as our first neighbors. They were the first White family who ever allowed their kids to play with us and the first White family Mom allowed me to visit when they invited us into their home. This man said my parents gave his family food and some cooking utensils when they first arrived in San Pedro because they had nothing and were very poor. They must have been more than poor. We were *poor*. They were *po' folk*.

He asked me if I remembered him, that we had played together as friends when his family first moved across the walk from my family. Our homes faced each other with only a walkway (not an alley between the back doors as in Dallas) that ran between the rows of little match box houses strategically placed up and down the slopes of the hill overlooking San Pedro Harbor. His family was the first White family I ever spoke to, looked into their eyes or played with. They pursued us as Mom cautiously allowed them to come and play on our small yard across the pavement from theirs. That line of demarcation was soon eradicated in their children's minds where a color barrier had not yet been established. This man, who now lives in Alabama with his family, reminded me that I chased him into his home because he hit my younger brother. What he had thought to be the truth all these years was a fabrication of his imagination. It was my older brother who policed my younger brother. He had recognized my name and image in national sporting events and tied me to my older brother's demand that he leave my younger brother alone. His call reminded me that people integrate, not institutions. My parents' kind gesture fanned a flame in the lamp of integration that civil rights activists had not yet achieved. I appreciated the call.

From segregated Dallas to integrating San Pedro was a loosening of the strangulation hold of oppression and fear which freed my curiosity to explore who I was to become. Everywhere I went in California there was a surrounding of White skin folk. They left me to work to improve upon being competitive in this world. Of course I know that there was still racism in San Pedro, but they didn't drive around at night *looking for a nigger to lynch.* My father and mother worked five days a week and we children went to school every day and kept our mouths shut. Church on Sunday was our weekly habit.

Early one morning on a beautiful day at the end of summer, we walked approximately three miles to the Barton Hill School to enroll, only to be told that our housing project was located outside that school's district. The next day we walked about four miles in a different direction up and down the hills along Gaffey Avenue to Cabrillo Avenue School, ready to enroll. After a most persuasive talk from our mother, we were finally admitted to Cabrillo. Almost instantly I was invited to play. The community of San Pedro had, without a doubt, the most profound impact on my life. The children covered in the skin of my most feared Southern enemy became my friends and associates and playmates. Within a few months, my life's course and destiny were shifted from oppression and the influence of people not wishing me well to that of people who let me be me. The power and freedom of choice taken from me at birth by a system of imposed racial preferences had been handed back to me. Oh, I know . . . it took more time than the twinkling of an eye to mature fully in its original intent and purpose, but less than half that time for the **seed of hope** to be planted in me. I'm convinced that racism is real, but most detrimental to those who harbor it.

My first and most dramatic experience was being accepted, not because of my color, but because of the outward manifestation of my soul's expression. It was there in the fourth and fifth grades, in the midst of being dodge-ball king, that I discovered that the combination of my hand-eye coordination, quickness, strength, intelligence and quick decision making skills was unique and would make me very competitive in the world which operated under the laws of supply and demand. I was on my way toward developing self confidence and self worth.

My fifth grade music appreciation teacher, whose name I believe was Mrs. Schuler and who looked like Mrs. See of candy fame, whispered in my ear one day, "Mr. Naulls, you have a very fine voice. *Keep up the good work. You can work at developing your God-given talent to the extent of your inner commitment.*" It's one of those encouraging phrases that get embedded in your memory and emerge at times of reflection like this.

My first fight was with the second biggest kid in the school, Big Marco. We shadow-boxed for a few minutes, never laying a hand on each other. I mention it because this was my first overt, aggressive act to defend myself against another person whose parents were covered in White skin.

My picture on the front page of the San Pedro News Pilot during fire drill day in the fifth grade, revealing that, compared to the rest of the student body at Cabrillo Avenue School, I was really large for my age; Mr. Schroeder's scolding the class for laughing at me when, given an opportunity to read before the class, I mispronounced the word "island" as "is-land"; not being able to sing with the fifth grade choir because I did not have the required black pants and white shirt to wear, and never telling Mrs. Schuler – nor my mother – why I had quit: These are memories which, for whatever reason or purpose, come up at this time on my heart's screen of events worth unpacking.

During those years from the third through the

fifth grade at Cabrillo Avenue School, I was liberated to compete individually against the entire school of White kids. I reigned as dodge ball king. From that beginning I developed increasing confidence in myself and my physical abilities and mental capabilities. Cabrillo's prominent teachers made indelible imprints on my soul. **Self worth based on merit alone is very important.**

Lesson: In athletic competition and in written and oral expression, White kids and Black kids were being evaluated from the inside-out rather than first from the outside appearance, which limits and influences individual growth by color.

In stark contrast, the last year of my grammar school experience was easily forgettable as students from the projects were cast out of Cabrillo Avenue School into the temporary bungalows of the Western Terrace Grammar School. It was an inferior school in every conceivable aspect of what a school's purpose is, and I believe that being in that environment retarded my educational development. The quality of the teachers was noticeably inferior in that they showed no interest in us personally. They gave us students the impression that they were substitutes until the real teachers showed up. The real teachers never did.

Lesson: A bad tree cannot produce good fruit; bad teachers cannot produce quality students.

The recreation playground in the center of Western Terrace was the outlet for the beginning of my development in sports. It had every kind of ball imaginable to be checked out with a signature, for as long as we wanted on any one day. Indoor badminton, outdoor basketball hoops , football field area, baseball diamonds near, punching bag, everything. I had never seen, heard of or imagined a recreation center before. This place became my home away from home and there I met my first coach, Coach Bob Wyrick who looked like Van Johnson of movie fame. He mobilized the Western Terrace kids to play on the first organized team that I experienced, competing against other parks in other areas of Southern California.

Selective memory takes me back now to when I first tried out for a baseball team at 11 years of age. The coach was called Coach "Oakie" and he looked like a Norman Rockwell character from the *Saturday Evening Post*. His face was bespeckled with brown spots highlighting his pale White skin. His teeth were "bucked" and cigarette stained *nasty* yellow. There was a part down the left side of his little peanut-shaped head. Outward protruding ears held his small circular steel-framed glasses in place and he oozed confidence. He methodically selected every White kid trying out for his Western Terrace Project team, choosing only one of the young boys covered with Black or Brown skin. After that rejection and throughout the months before the next season's tryouts, I threw a baseball all winter long at a skillet, thinking of his face. I mounted it on the center post of the backstop directly behind home plate. Past nightfall the surrounding neighbors heard the gong as my fast balls registered on target. The next year, we Black and Brown skinned "Oakie" rejects beat his team 15-0 and 25-2 in the two league games we played. He had the unmitigated gall to ask me and others whom he had rejected the season before to play for him. Later that season I pitched my only no-run, no-hit game in the regional championship game. So the foundation was already laid solidly to understand that coaches had the power of subjective rejection of me because of my skin color. To move on past that subjective rejection of my talent by coaches before and during high school was a challenge which weighed me down mentally. It was my choice to just say No and move on past the attempts of White men to discourage me by placing inferiorly talented White-skinned players on their team rosters ahead of me. Solely because their moms and dads were covered with White skin, they were given preference. My mom and dad were covered with Black skin and coaches would have to live with the fact that I was very comfortable being a young man covered with Black skin. I was always ready to say, *Let's get it on!* By the rules of the game, of course. These coaches' sole purpose appeared to be to discourage me with unfair use of their authority. Their agenda was to have me become the fulfillment of their vision for all those who looked like me, to give up and scream *foul.*

Much of what has been taught to me in my life which I consider to be of profound truth only repeats what was told to me by my mother. Her message implanted itself in my young, fertile soil: *"You have a great gift from God, son: the freedom of choice. Choose the journey of life and not death."* **Lesson: Whatever you do that is done to promote God's Word of life – and not death – is good and is honored by God.**

The move from the stifling governmental system of the South to the less oppressive one of the west identified a freedom in me that my mom already had by faith under Biblical doctrine. God has given everyone the power of choice. He has commanded those who choose Him to choose life, that they and their seed may live. These very words inspired me to persevere in a world which suppressed and oppressed people of my skin color. I chose not to be of that world and its negative philosophy about who I AM. I declared with others of like precious faith that my days of living in this life are long upon the earth – and my seed lives to prosper because I choose to listen to and act upon God's words taught me by my mother and my teachers. God's message of liberation is Empowered Choice.

I AM WHAT I AM.

I AM What I AM

". . . by the grace of God, I am what I am,
and His grace to me was not without effect."
I Corinthians 15:10

When you see,
Do you really see Me?
And, when you hear,
Do you really hear through to Me?
Way inside what you see as Me
Is a voice to be seen as Me and heard
as Me.
I am more than what you see or hear Me
to be.
For I am!

More than perception
    And conception
Of what appears to Be,
I am Me!

Hear Me and know that I am
    Real -
And see Me through seeing -
    Not through sense alone,
        But, by Faith, as Being.
Real, eternal Me.

I am, more than sight alone,
    But Seeing -
See through to Me, for
I AM what I AM In Christ
    Who Empowers Me
    To be Me.

I AM what I AM.
". . . by the grace of God,
I AM what I AM,
and His grace to me
was not without effect."
I AM what I AM!

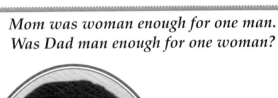

**Mom was woman enough for one man.
Was Dad man enough for one woman?**

Daily and Bettie Naulls

The Roaring '20s

Indelible Lesson on My Soul:
Surviving Abuse on the Path to Independence

I give credit to my parents, Bettie Arlene Naulls and Daily Lovejoy Naulls, for raising me to go in the direction they thought would be in my best interest. Mom taught moral **Lessons** both verbally and by example. Dad went to work every day, rain or shine, on time (as did Mom), branding in the hides of their children that there was no excuse for being late or not honoring your word to show up to work. **"Honor your word."** Dad's and Mom's voices echoed in my actions through to my children. As a central theme of our Southern training, they also thought it important that their children stand erect with eyes forward, never looking into the eyes of any person, especially those covered with White skin. Dad managed money well. "Saving for a rainy day" was stressed, and our family paid off every contract that he and Mom ever committed to.

However, I never liked or respected my father very much because of the things he imposed upon my mother, sister and me. His actions demonstrated to his children that he thought it all right to lie and cheat and disrespect one's wife, and he on occasion beat Mom to within an *inch* of her life. He imposed on his family *"Daily's strife."* "Do as I say and not as I do" was his unspoken creed. I survived and my mother endured – that I might have a better life. She **living trusted** me with God's Holy advice. But my sister was helpless in slaughter as he did violate his own daughter. *To Hell he Fell*, but God's grace he openly would sell before his demise. In a moment of confrontation, God's Word pulled out of my stow His meaning of forgiveness for me to grow. Judgment is mine, came His Sovereign Voice, so cleanse your soul of lamenting his choice. When I tallied to weigh my force, a poem emerged to alter my course:

Did You Ever Wish?

Did you ever wish you had a dad
the thought of whom didn't make you sad?
A father whose memories made you inside
    to smile
giving you inner peace being there all the
    while?

Idealistic I know to think this way
'cause "truth's in the puddin'" as do "they
    say"

But what a relief, if in his tracks to trek
in all our anxious moments when satan's
    messengers did beck?
If dad could have been there as our light to
    guide
little feet through tough decisions, holding
    my hand by his side

But that's not possible, to reach back and
    change
Only in fantasy can imagination rearrange
that profound and lasting imprint
a father's decision makes during his stint

He is the male image to a child so grand
the early model of manhood by which to
    stand

What do I say to young folk, as God's
    Messenger on Call?
Whom to recommend as a role model for
    their hearts to install?
Thank God He's given me the answer, with
    no shadow to shift
Anchor your heart in the Lord Jesus, and
    don't let Him drift

The interwoven experiences of my life have
given me uniqueness as a flower, bloomed of those
seeds of **Lessons**.

What was the beginning of my father's rage
    planting?
Who introduced the thought of his mind's
    engranting?
Deep into the mire where jealousy is mixed
came a sowing suggestion of adultery –
    fixed

I remember the night very clearly, as I peeked
from under the sheet which covered me. I saw,
through a partially opened door, a man – not my
father – trying to kiss my mother in the next
room. His knock on the front door had awakened
me and their voices had inspired my curiosity.
Before she closed the door between the rooms he
had tried to embrace her, but she pushed him away
and asked him to leave. My little radio was tuned to

The Shadow which aired between seven and eight o'clock. *Inner Sanctum*, the next fear-expanding radio program whose ending we never heard, was airing so it was somewhere between eight and nine when I heard the front door close. Mom came into our room and turned off the radio. I was relieved to fall back into the peace of her good night kiss on my cheek and her protection alone, for Dad was off to World War II obligations.

From Under the Covers, I Spy

From under the covers, I spy
innocent images, they do die
unfaithful mother? No way! I cry
daddy's at war, we sigh
he set the standard, then good-bye
From under the covers, I spy

From under the covers, I spy
innocent images, they do die
real life drama through the eye
injected into the heart, arrows fly
wicked deceptions panned to fry
cooking rage of jealousy in G.I.
From under the covers, I spy

From under the covers, I spy
innocent images, they do die
brother harboring, same as I
the unspeakable scene, he thought to try
tapping daddy's love, admitting its
    innocence, to buy
From under the covers, I spy

From under the covers, I spy
innocent images, they do die
rage of jealousy – pointing – in finger's
cry
thumb points back at him, in
retribution's mire
for all the adultery that he did conspire
leading a good woman down that slope
he humiliated her soul, unable to cope
From under the covers, I spy

From under the covers, I spy
innocent images, they do die
years later, as I walked this way
I saw dear ol' dad coming out that day
from the adulterous den, he scoffed to
say
as I looked upon the face of her that day
"What are you doing around here, boy?
Get on your way."
From under the covers, I spy

From under the covers, I spy
innocent images, they do die
when I responded with the truth, he
said, "you lie"
my relationship with dad was never the
same
he preferred my brother in their
confession game
my mom, she would suffer the wrath of
his rage
which my brother's *loyalty* let out of its
cage
From under the covers, I spy

From under the covers, I spy
innocent images they do die
to snarl and spit on her – and me too
like we were animals in his private zoo
he beat her body, trying to relieve his
        pain
knowing that he was the one who was
        rendered insane
oh, to move on and live each hour
as preciously strong in the strength of a
        flower
created by God, unique and of worth
in the sole purpose of Him, who gave
        me birth
From under the covers, I spy

From under the covers, I spy
innocent images, they do die
forgiving is better than cancerous
        restraint
harboring the choices of others in daily
        complaint
get the Life which has abundantly come
whose love doesn't care where you've
        come from
not as the world's temporarily offered
        its peace
His Peace is everlasting, never to cease
From under the covers, I spy

I never discussed with my brother whether he witnessed or what he thought of Mom's encounter that Sunday night in Dallas, Texas, which was interpreted as adulterous a couple of years later, in a different place, San Pedro, California. My father's face was demanding and intimidating when he confronted me to verify what my brother had *given up* during interrogations about my mother's activities while he was away in the war effort. I told him that I didn't see my mother do anything with any man. He challenged me, asking if I thought my brother were lying. "Either he's lying or you're hiding something." I told him I wasn't lying and didn't know what my brother was talking about. He was furious and told me that he had thought I was an honest son but now he knew that I wasn't. He forced the issue by advancing toward me. For the first time, we had a *stare down*, negotiating our positions from two vantage points: his perceived and self-proclaimed power position from the moment of my birth and my maturing oneness to be a man, independent of him. A smack on the side of my head released the cement of rebellion to flow into my inner forming foundational blocks. I looked at him with camouflaged rage through my non-shifting eyes. I said, "You can hit me all you want but I didn't see Mama do anything." Three more slaps – then silence – then his life directional dismissal of me: "Get on out of my sight, boy!"

I had not been present at my brother's inter-rogation and can only surmise that it had been equally intense. Until this moment, I never thought about forgiving either of them for their collusion to assuage my father's insane desire to put out the fire of not knowing the details of my mother's life when he wasn't home. From that day his entire attitude changed. He sauntered into every family situation with out of control babbling about wives who played around on their husbands – wives who couldn't be trusted. He used words that I knew were bad even before I knew what they meant. In shell shock, Mom retreated in embarrassment before her children and neighbors as Dad's voice grew in intensity and volume. Up to that point in our family's growing up together, we were a quiet, church-going group of five, minus my *rolling stone* father. I never saw my father hold my mother in his arms nor heard him tell her that he loved her. He never told me that he loved me, but I rationalized that to be all right at the time. He only spoke demeaning and vulgar words followed by hostile threats. He spent increasingly longer evenings away from home as the distance between him and my mother and me grew. I don't know how my younger brother and sister reacted to Dad at that time because I also spent more and more time away from home. I was busy honing my mind and body at school and participating in athletics, living the acculturation of integrating skin colors. Dad soon erupted from hostile words to overflowing physical violence against my mom.

Dragged away by the intent of entice
the tempter lured my father through
    jealousy's advice
Embracing evil's desire he did conceive
sin unto death that only Christ could
    relieve.

I was awakened one night by screams from

the center space of our three-room rented govern-
ment housing project home on the southern side of a
hill overlooking the Pacific Ocean port of San Pedro,
California. Immediately, my two brothers were off
the upper bunk of our army issue double deck
sleeping beds and at the door. I reached to uncoil
my feet which were entangled in the Army surplus
blanket which kept them warm. My body extended
off the end of the six-foot bed which was not long
enough to support my 6' 2", 12 year old frame. As
we emerged through the door, we saw my father
straddling my mother on the floor, hitting her with
the full force of his rage, in her face and on her body.
He drove and drove his fist – and rested – and
drove, his anger surging. Then he turned on us,
challenging our screams with threats to kick our
butts if we didn't get back in our room and close the
door. When we hesitated, he charged the door,
swinging and lunging and cursing – then a loud
slam – and then the sound of his footsteps running
after my mother out the front door.

Where was my sister of nine years of age? We
three sat there in the dark room in obedience to his
threats for what seemed like hours, in silence and
mental suffering. *Why didn't I give my life to protect
Mom from him? How can I ever forgive myself? I'll get
him one of these days!* I thought to myself. Fear took
a deeper grip into my soul – even greater than that
of the *Boogie Man* – for that legendary figure had a
bodily form now – and he looked like my dad.

Suddenly our attention was drawn to the sounds
of multiple footsteps approaching the front door,
across the threshold, beyond that same space of my
mother's screams for help, pleading: **"Dale, please
don't kill me," Mom** pained! **"Please don't kill**

me!" A police officer opened the door to our room and flooded his flashlight into our eyes. "You boys all right?" Our neighbor had called them right on time. My dad was physically subdued by the authorities who shut down the flood of his invading insane frenzy. My mom, at our attention diverting moment, had escaped with my sister out the front door and into the home of one of our neighbors. Soon thereafter and through a mounting crowd of all White neighbors, she came back into the house and ran to us. She bundled my younger brother in her arms, looking up from her 5′ 5 1/2″ battered frame into the eyes of my older brother and myself, asking if we were okay. With swollen and bloodshot eyes, she lamented with words over her severely split lips that her first concern was her children.

When two other officers came to our door with my father *in hand*, they asked her if she wanted them to take him to jail for the abuse he had inflicted on her. She hesitated at the sound of Dad's plea, "Arlene, please don't let them take me to jail. I didn't mean it. Arlene . . . ." The officers asked her firmly, "Mrs., do you want us to take him to jail for what he's done to you?" She began to cry profusely and finally said, "Yes, I do want you to take him away so he won't hurt my children." It was one of those moments you can't erase from your memory: three officers of the law dragging my wailing father out the door into a paddy wagon and off to jail. His eyes were full of fear and submission to the final civil authority – the PO′ – LICE! *Bad boy, sick man, what's your plan; what's your plan now that they've called your hand?*

Years before San Pedro, the civil authority in Dallas, Texas, might never have responded to a

woman covered with Black skin's plea for her life
and her civil and human rights, to be protected from
her husband's violence. But we were away from
that Southern Black-on-Black-in-Black society. My
parents had intentionally moved us into the midst of
a community where Black was surrounded by White
neighbors. That's not a popular way to think these
days; nevertheless it's evidence of the evolving civil
rights of Choice.

The officers of the law put sufficient fear in my
father over the next few weeks behind bars to
release in him a higher respect for and obedience to
the laws protecting women and victims. Our home
was quiet when he wasn't there and I really liked
that. My mother healed on the outside but we were
all left for the rest of our lives together holding our
breath, expecting the beast in him to Dr. Hyde us at
any moment. Pain, Pain, Pain – is Fear – Insane.

Never, ever, I thought, will I hit a woman – and
especially not my wife. Years later I did – once – slap
a woman in the fit of an enraged male macho jealous
insanity let out of its cage. But I immediately
apologized in earnestness of repentance. Mercifully
she didn't summon that same authority to
incarcerate me.

When I was in my thirties I asked my mother if
she wanted me to care for her. I offered to have her
come to live with me in my home and away from
Dad's ongoing threats and verbal abuse which had
continued from that night. She said, "Thank you,
but no thanks." Her answer was perplexing to
me at the time because I always assumed that she
was so miserable with him that she was eagerly
looking to escape his influence. I asked why she had
put up with him all those years. She said in her soft,

Mom and Dad
A life together they had
from a distance – real sad
bonded as one – so clad

Bettie and Daily Naulls

convincing voice through a smile from her heart, "I guess I love him, William. I do love him!" *Until death do us part* took on a new meaning.

The **Lesson** made clear to me was that I needed to *find a girl, just like the girl that married dear ol' dad* – and to love her as Christ loves His church.

The potential confusion of living in a home divided was always defused by my mom's commitment to not contend against my father's authority but to work together with, and under duress from, my father. Her mission was to raise up her children in the way God would have them go. To her, forgiveness of my father was as Biblically commanded as "seventy times seven" – and more. Even the pride in adultery was defeated by her acts of encircling love. Why did she give up her life for me? She gave me her answer to that question by encouraging me to meditate on what God teaches in Scripture? Why did Christ Jesus give up His life for the sin of all of us? She taught me that when she took up her cross to follow after Jesus, He gave her life to testify: "I guess I love you, William. I do love you, William." The **Lesson** that I learned here is that **MOM LOVED ME!** To endure it all was her call.

Empathic Ode of an Unaborted Soul

**A tribute to all mothers who chose not to
murder the Life at conception within them,
and who chose to give up the responsibility
of that developing child to others**

I know I'm supposed to be
God gave me life to see
His Vision through my Mom set free
whose **Spirit** stood against aborting me
In unrest, I have never known
her bosom of love, now I'm grown
I yearn to thank her, to share in her pain
of what she shoulders, not knowing my
     name,
in giving me up to a pro-life plan
She relieved her young burden to scan
the freedom of choice, minus the respon-
     sibility
of the life conceived, unwanted in me
But my offer to you, Mom, wherever you
     live
is the love of the Lord Jesus, who does
     forgive
He's cleansed me of hatred which I
     embraced about you
and gave me His freedom to know that
     God loves you too

And whatever your decision, Mom, of
    years long ago,
submit to His will and join our family to
    know
that God in His Son loved the world so
    much
that whoever believes in Him sheds sin's
    heavy clutch
So, I know I'm supposed to be
God gave me life to see
His Vision through my Mom set free
whose **Spirit** stood against aborting me
Through believing, I am as He
'cause as He Is I will to be

Mom's blessing to me taught me to be a blessing
to others – my wife and my children. Human logic
says that the inner logic of interpersonal relationships would have us clueless as to why my mother
chose to stay the course with my father, who was so
insensitive and so abusive. God's Logic/His
Wisdom would say through my mother's actions of
loving and never forsaking her family:

> *"For my thoughts are not your thoughts,*
> *neither are your ways my ways," declares*
> *the Lord. "As the heavens are higher than*
> *the earth, so are my ways higher than your*
> *ways and my thoughts than your thoughts."*
>   Isaiah 55:8-9

Yes, God has given me my wife, Anne, who is
the girl, just like the girl who married dear ol' dad.
As another song inspires, once I found her, I must
love her so that she will never want to go.

My father was eventually let out of the cage in which justice had placed him for his term. He returned home determined to reestablish his rule of our family hierarchy. Under my mother's leadership, we had in fact developed into a smoothly running cooperative. Under her direction, we four children, with her, did everything better and more efficiently and in love while he was away. Dad's first *power trip* was silence, which we ignored. Then he tried isolation of affection from my mom. He gave special rewards for loyalty to my older brother by conversing with him before anyone else. The only time he spoke to me was through a disapproving command. His attempts to demean me influenced me further and further into my isolationist position of independence. I thought, *Hey, ol' man – I don't need you, and as soon as I'm through high school, I'm out of here.*

On school and work days, Dad drove his family of six to the bus stop in his 1941 two-door Pontiac. We disembarked at the corner of 6th and Front Streets across from the Channel Island Ferry Building. Mom took the bus from there out to Point Fermin where she worked for Dr. and Mrs. Thompson and their two children. Lois Thompson was my classmate in junior high and high school. I sometimes wondered when I looked into her eyes whether she felt blessed to know my mother, who loved, cared for, cooked and cleaned for her and her brother as she did for us. We kids took separate buses to our school locations. En route to our bus stop, my dad appeared angry most of the time. When he stopped for gas the station's attendant asked, "May I help you, sir?"

"A dollar wurff of ethyl," he asked for daily in a

low voice, as he always bought the highest grade of gasoline for his main thrill, his Pontiac Chief.

"What's that, sir? I didn't hear you."

"A DOLLAR WURFF OF ETHYL!" Dad roared, his voice loud enough to be heard across the street. The attendant, after putting the gas in the car and the cap back in place, had seconds to come and get payment or my dad would, on occasion, throw the money out the window and drive off.

He was still establishing himself, through his hostile antics, as undisputed boss of our family. All of us, including Mom, had conceded power to him, but he acted as though it were his life or death work. I knew that his power to influence me was absolute, but it was limited and had a definite *closing date*. So I tolerated and ignored his insanity. Empathically and retrospectively, I believe my father was a victim of the hand he had been dealt in east Texas. Racism had imposed restrictions on him because of his Black skin. Born as one of 19 brothers, sisters, step-brothers and step-sisters on a farm somewhere between Texarkana and Marshall, he never went to school past the third grade. He never shared with us what he did as a youth or teenager; but his reputation, I surmised after I was old enough to hear comments and observe reactions to him, was that of a ladies' man who wanted to be an unimpeded *rolling stone*.

Somewhere in his deeper self I assume he must have felt responsible for his children. He worked **Daily** to provide us with a place to live and food to eat. His instinct toward male dominance and ultimate responsibility drove him to be accountable and to pay his bills on time. We were taught not to ask anyone for anything. "If you don't work for what you get, it's not worth having" were his words. His position on working for what you get was the force in me which screamed to be independent from his rule and authority. Shouting from the top of his convictions, he voiced his final word on his authority, "If you don't like what's going on around here, there's the door. This is the house that Daily rules. No other voice but mine is final *in any decision* made in this place that I pay for."

Ostensibly that extreme position reduced my mother to a 40-hour/$40 per week domestic who, in addition to working for others, cooked all the meals at our home, including breakfast and dinner every day, seven days a week; but she didn't feel that way. With a smile on her face and a song in her heart, she kept our home spotless, training all of us to be responsible for ourselves as her assistants. She did all our washing, sewing, and soothing even as she took Dad's abusing. She was the underappreciated, devoted and unwavering wife to Daily Naulls.

During our rides in the Pontiac, I learned to drive by watching my father maneuver and coordinate the clutch with the gear shift which was mounted under the steering wheel. He was a very smooth driver most of the time but when his mental attitude was bad, it directly affected his driving. My mom, who sat in the middle of the front seat, always reminded me when she did not approve of Dad's maneuvering in traffic. Her elbow bore deeply into my ribs whenever she was the most affected. Over time she literally wore a hole in the mat under her feet, *back-seat-driving*, gesturing to help Dad stop before we got too close to another car.

Because of my height I always got the front right
window seat. My older brother, who was six inches
shorter than I, sat in the back with my younger twin
brother and sister. I never thought about how he
must have felt, but after I became a father driving
our family of six around, deciding who would sit
where and for what reason, I empathized with my
dad's challenge. It was my height that secured my
position in the front seat. But how did my brother
feel, being the eldest, sitting in the back seat looking
at the back of my head during those few years of our
growing up together? The point here is that we
Naulls children had no empathy for one another.
We rode in silence, eager to be dropped off and away
from each other.

   After all these years, I still don't know who my
older brother was during that time. I thought that
he was considered a better athlete and student than
I. I don't remember my brother congratulating me
for my athletic achievements. Did he wish me well?
It was hard to tell, 'cause we never did gel. Very few
people knew how great was his potential because he
never extended himself in sports and evolved to be
the school's African American *pretty boy*. His clothes
always looked the sharpest, his shoes were always
the shiniest and his hair was always the *groomiest*. I
did not know his friends nor did he know mine. We
were in different worlds at the same schools and just
a year and a half separated us by grades. We talked
more as we grew older but that only revealed
further the fact that we were virtual strangers. I told
him I loved him a couple of years ago and he just
looked shocked and did not respond. Too little – too
late? A definition of faith is . . . perceiving as real fact
what is not revealed to the senses. Both of us could

learn from Mom's example – to love one another by
Faith . . . perceiving love as real fact even though we
don't sense it.

Dramatically impacting our lives during that
time were our cousins on our dad's side. They
migrated from Domino, Texas, to San Pedro about
two years after our family. My father's sister's son,
Cousin Felix McGilvery, had gotten a job through
my dad at Todd Shipyard. The great impact that
his wife, Cousin Dessie, had on my life is   that
she believed in me. One memorable day she
demonstrated her faith in me by speaking up on my
behalf. In an area used for parking and washing cars behind our cousin's home in mid-Saturday
morning, my father was preparing his beloved but
aging Pontiac to be sold. I washed the old relic as
my dad verbally expressed that he wanted to paint
a for-sale sign on the rear side windows but didn't
have a brush. I stepped forward and told him, "I
can do it, Dad."

He said to me in a firm voice, "Get back, boy!
You can't do anything right and you never will be
able to do anything right."

My cousin Dessie spoke up, stopping my
mother's words in their tracks: "Daily, you should
be ashamed of yourself talking to William like that.
He can do anything better than any of you Naullses
and one of these days, if you are not careful, all of
you will be looking to him to feed you. William,
paint the sign on the car your own way." Dad,
uncharacteristically, took several steps backward,
away from the car. I picked up a rag and the can of
paint, wrapped the rag around a stick, dipped the
improvised brush into the can and painted "FOR

SALE" very neatly in block letters on the two rear side windows.

As I closed the can and folded the rag to dispose of it in the trash, I looked in the eyes of my cousin, thanking her as my self control almost yielded to the joy of encouragement mounting in my heart. My mother said, "Excellent job, Baby." Cousin Dessie said, "You can do anything you set your mind to. Don't let anybody tell you you can't." These two women's eyes *growled* in my father's direction. Cousin Felix, his son (Cousin Mac, my basketball hero and mentor who was three years older than I), his three daughters – Dessie, Dorothy and Raye – and my two brothers observed in silence as these two important women spoke words of encourage-ment into me. The will of God was expressed through them to me and not the will of the one who influenced my dad – and that dog in him who chased the cat toward its cornering. Didn't my own father wish me well? With that possibility always present in my mind, I was well prepared to not expect any empathy from coaches or teammates. Those who judge performance of any kind where objective rather than subjective evaluations are required face my father's dilemma. I have learned that **Truth** is integrity's foundation.

> Integrity is always being able to count on me
> to do whatever God's **Truth** does decree
> 'cause that's the only way my soul is set free

That was an important cumulative **Lesson** taught to me that day: Adults can encourage and train – or they can discourage and disdain – young minds. Daily living was preparing me to make wise choices in any situation which might come up from time to time. We were all in the arena of the **Truth** in sociological family and community development through lived experiences. My father wasn't my enemy! My enemy was the voice whom he listened to. How did I know? My mom told me that whoever said I was no good was acting out the devil's orders. I don't know how these common experiences affected the rest of my family's will to work at becoming God's created best, but I am the fruit of those **Lessons'** seed plantings. I was really fired up by that experience to face the next challenge in my life.

All of us displaced Texans at my cousin's house that day were about three blocks from the front entrance of the recreation center which was in the middle of our housing project. The harbor was in plain view from there but our families spent very little time observing the incredible beauty from that vantage point. Seaport Drive was a two-lane road running from its dead end on the northeast toward the southwest and ended at the only street exit for the residents. The northern boundary of the homes abutted what we thought to be one of the state's largest and most productive oil refineries.

We were awakened early one morning by a massive explosion. The ensuing fire and loud alarms brought panic upon everyone to immediately leave the hillside by foot or car. The fallout from the inferno of burning oil and gas was smothering and choking and life threatening. When our family car was able to get onto the main road out, it took what seemed to be a lifetime for us to get to the bottom of the hill. The long stream of cars moving one way in both lanes downhill were packed with anxious faces and families who had left their homes behind, carrying only their bare necessities. At the bottom of the hill, there was a choice to turn either to the left from that point going east and north toward Wilmington and Los Angeles or to the right around the shipyard on the route Dad normally took to our bus stop each morning.

When Dad left us off that morning, we were early for our buses and had time to reflect as we looked back toward our home on the side of the hill and the fire and smoke in the background. Mom was clearly the calming force as she assured us that God was right there with us to protect us. We had a choice to trust Him and be calm or to panic. She didn't mention Dad, but we knew that he was included in her remarks, for he had definitely panicked. The explosion occurred at about five in the morning, an hour before we normally awakened to get ready for school. Mom was already up and preparing biscuits for breakfast. When the blast reverberated, my father's initial cry was to the Lord. Mom had to comfort him and help him calm down and find his "stuff." His insecurities flared up when he was stressed. We kids were up and dressed in minutes waiting for instructions. We had been trained by our mother to get ready for each day the night before, so we were ready. We looked to her and she prayed, "God will take care of us. Help your father get ready. God will protect us off this mountain." During that slow trip down the southern side of the hill where the Western Terrace housing project was developed, her voice in prayer – and then her distracting comments about the new paint job on the recreation center, her compliment to

Under the same roof we did dwell
but I never knew them very well
Three years seemed a lifetime betwixt
twin souls and mine – never time to mix

Geraldine and Jerry Naulls

Age 5 years
Dallas, Texas

me about the good job I was doing cutting and trimming the yards we passed – taught me the importance of trusting in God when in danger zones. **Self control, patience and perseverance** were maturing in me. As we left the car in silence, my father did not even look our way as we all said, "Goodbye, Dad."

A few days passed before there was total control and cleanup of the refinery *next door*, but the Naulls family compound was uneasy. The cover had been pulled from my father, exposing his fears and insecurities. He did not act as though he believed that God was Sovereign in our lives. My mom asked God to be Sovereign in our lives and He was. Dad began to treat her with increased hostility, to which she responded with assurance that she would not tolerate physical violence from him ever again. The threat of the PO-LICE was always on his mind so he was reluctant to cross the line from his verbal, vulgar, demeaning speech to physical violence. His antics were grievous to her soul and we kids suffered with her.

When I arrived home one evening, without so much as one private word with me, Mom dropped the bombshell that she was going back to Dallas, taking my younger brother and sister with her. She said that she was confident that my older brother and I could take care of ourselves. I knew that she had heard or seen with her own eyes, as I had, that Dad had other female interests. She said, "Your father doesn't want me any more."

It's difficult to explain the pain of watching her departure the next day. I stood on the side of that same southern hillside viewing large ships docked in Todd Shipyard and the Pacific Ocean in

Thoughts of my older brother, Bill,
provoke my subconscious still.
Why doesn't my mind just chill
when I know it's the Lord's will?

Bill Naulls

Age 9 years
Dallas, Texas

the background. My brother and I watched as our mother and our younger sister and brother boarded the Red Car headed for Union Station to catch the train to Texas. I wanted to cry and moan and wail, but at my side was my brother who took it all in stride. So I packed it in for another day, another incident. My father had pushed her to her limits and now she was Dallas-bound. When we arrived back home, we found Dad eating a can of sardines and crackers. He looked up and then back down at his food for a moment. He said, "You boys are going to have to take care of yourselves now. I'm not going to cook or clean for you or wash your clothes or any of that. Your mama left you and you're on your own. Don't ask me for nothing." He then got up, got his hat and walked out. My brother followed him out the door.

I was on my own. The tears came, washing away the lumps of melting pain. Suddenly I felt a surge of independence. I remembered that I had a Pet Milk can bank full of fifty-cent coins I had saved from my lawn cutting business. Mom's final words, "I trust you to take care of yourself," reminded me of the **Lessons** she had taught me: the importance of personal hygiene, how to wash and iron my own clothes, etc. Through assisting her I knew how to cook. She taught me that a part of self respect was to clean up after myself. I knew where to shop for food and whatever else I needed. The challenge was that I would have to find a new barber to replace Dad as I felt uncomfortable asking anything of my father. I didn't want him to think that I needed him for anything. My older brother lived under the same roof, but I don't remember ever talking to him about anything during that period.

On a day when I arrived home from baseball practice with some groceries that I had purchased with some of my "stash," my dad, looking up from his plate of food, appeared shocked. He demanded to know where I had gotten the food and I told him I had bought it with some of my money. "Have you been stealing or begging, boy? Where did you get that food?" he yelled.

In disbelief, I didn't say anything but just stared at him. He yelled again, demanding an answer. I repeated my answer, pointing toward the location of my hidden Pet Milk can bank. He demanded that I get it and be prepared to tell him where I had gotten the money. I set the bag of groceries on the sink counter, went into my room, brought out the can and gave it to him. He said, "Where did you get this money from?"

"From cutting *my customers'* yards every week," I told him firmly. I named the people and told him that he could go and ask them since he didn't believe me. He leaped from his chair and smacked me on the side of my head and reminded me that he was still *the man in charge* around his house, so don't get smart with my answers. I stared at him again in silence, noticing that I was looking him directly in the eyes. I also remember at that moment his words to me about who was boss and if I didn't like that, to get my own place and pay my own rent. *Pay the cost to be the boss.*

"How long have you been doing these yards and what have you been doing with the money?" I told him that for a couple of years I had been giving some of my money to Mama to help buy our food and to help buy clothes and shoes for us. By his facial expression, he seemed embarrassed and surprised. He even looked disappointed that I wasn't the thief and beggar he postulated me to be. After a pregnant silence, he said, "I'll keep this here can and from now on you bring anything you make to me and I'll buy the groceries around here; do you understand, boy?"

"Yes, sir," I said, staring past his unsteady eyes to the pallet in the back of his throat. Was it time to dishonor my father? Was he living up to the standard of a parent deserving honor as taught me by my mom? He was exasperating me and that was against God's commandments, but Mom had said to honor and forgive him. His words and smack on the side of my head were reverberating inside the *I AM* in me as he went back around the table to sit down beside my silent brother. He took my money and never discussed with me how he spent my Pet Milk can bank full of fifty cent coins; nor did I ask!

Behind a closed door, in my room alone, I sat in the silence of where I do hear my own questions and answers. *He took all of my money!* Truly, this was someone that I did not want to be associated with. I thought, *Who is the thief here?* I believed at that moment that my brother was collaborating with this person who had caused my mother so much pain and had forced her resolve to leave us. He appeared not to understand. I decided that I would never ask my father for a dime or a morsel of food. I would rather have died than depend on him, or anyone else for that matter. My ship left shore under my own mental power of independence that day. My father tried on many occasions to give me a token gift to get me back into his power influence, but I refused. He never asked me for my earnings again and even ate some of the food I purchased out of my second and third Pet Milk can banks. As a teenager I was already living the prophetic word of my Cousin Dessie – feeding my family. Of course, that line of thought is a stretch.

When You Cry, You Cry Alone?

Somehow my soul never quite grew
    beyond
as unknowingly I embraced the devil's
    con
that through my father's hostile rejection
    of me
it caused my heart to cower –my soul
    yearning to be free
Whenever do we take the time to think
as the doing of life flashes in the blur of a
    blink
stammering – who am I and how can I
    protect myself to survive
outside the *best nest* of the – *people needing*
    people –– contrive?
In the worst of times – when the razor's
    edge cut so deep
I cried out of tears – alone – no one could
    hear me weep
Nobody looked deep enough to ask,
    "How you feeling inside?"
Stud in appearance caused relationships
    to glide
Weaving in between – I never quite got a
    fix
in the mortar of living – just past in
    betwixt

Everybody thought, He can handle it,
  which ostensibly I did
as the shallowness inside relationships
  continuously slid
Then one day amid a mid morning's
  surprise
LOVE's intervention awakened my
  dormant spiritual eyes
thawing the cell block of self protection
  retrofitted in me
the **Truth** foundation promised emerged
  and set me free
In the best of times – now – the tears of
  joy overflowing
out of the abundance of **Christ's Life's
  Seed** sowing
exposed the **Crying Alone** agenda as a
  promotion of lies
because Christ Jesus lives with me, even
  after my body dies

My mother was lured by my father back from Dallas about a year later. She was a stranger whom I received in the same caution of self-protecting my inner feelings as I did my dad. The advantage of her position in my life for both of us was that she had taught me the **Lessons** which sustained me while she was away, I believed, to stay. My life had changed dramatically, for I had entered the world of athletics. At every level of competition, I was the most honored. I worked and studied and played sports through junior high and high school, becoming more and more independent with every passing day. It was me against every *other* in the world. I was always down on the spiritual line of scrimmage, poised to protect and advance my position.

Longshoremen, with whom I did day work from the age of 12 during summer months unloading giant cargo ships, told my father what a great athlete I was developing into. He confronted me, shouting that he was embarrassed that all of the men on his job knew about my talent while he didn't. He had never seen me play sports because he was more interested in what he did than in me. He had demonstrated over the years that he had no confidence in my ability to do anything. Mom instilled in me the confidence to be who she thought God had created me to be. She taught me that it was up to me to develop into me. "Take care of yourself, William, 'cause no one else should have to." If not for Mom, I might have been a recycling pain in Dad's sorry image – to living trust that curse on to my wife and children.

I made a shocking discovery one evening after a long day of school and after-school athletic practice. My bank had been *robbed*. It never occurred to me that Mom could be wrong. She had assured me that my relatives could be trusted, especially the ones with whom I slept and ate in a place called home. In the south, I had been taught that my relatives could be trusted. When some violated family trust they were scorned and ostracized. At home I lived in the privacy of my own thoughts in my small space of one-third share of a bedroom. There was always in me a burning desire for real privacy – to know for sure that people left my things untouched and non-violated when I was away from home. My bank had been robbed! I was speechless and almost out of breath as I looked down into the eyes of my mom as I approached the sink where she was preparing dinner. She called everyone into the room and demanded to know who the thief was. No one confessed so I suspected them all. My father wasn't there until later and I heard from my room his *final answer* to my crisis: "I told the boy to bring what he earned to me for safe keeping. Serves him right!" I felt so violated and didn't speak or relate to my brothers and sister earnestly ever again. I again questioned, *Who was the thief?* Soon I had savings again but never inside the house. I buried my treasure *under* our house, and most times I needed additional cans for my lawn cutting business was flourishing. When I left home to fulfill my UCLA scholarship, I carried with me a few hundred dollars to establish my own bank account in a real bank in Westwood Village, USA. The walls of that final *miff* about blood being thicker than water eroded and washed away into another true life's **Lesson**: "The love of money is the root of all evil."

The love of money's **Lesson** rooted in me and I guard my trust in mankind until this day. Very few, if any, people know of my financial worth. I learned to trust my wife, Anne, even before we were married and we instructed all of our children to understand that *money is The Tempter* and it is wise to never display valuables openly and to put them in a safe place.

Upon reflection, I realized that I was guilty of being a thief even before my *bank robbery*. Way back in Dallas, I had taken nickels and dimes which did not belong to me and had stolen candy and cookies from stores, even though I knew it was wrong. The love of money has many faces. He can be seen in a theft of office supplies at one's workplace or in cheating on taxes or on school examinations, in not returning an overpayment of change at a store, in not sharing that part of a commission belonging to another, in the actions of those who violate the law in insider trading, in exploiting the public through contrived inner circle bonus plans, through creating demand by controlling and limiting supply, and so on. And what about not giving honor where honor is due, before the press, to those who assist you, improving their exposure to get recognition, better jobs and abundance for their families? Beware of a man who talks, but doesn't walk "not being concerned about who gets the credit" if he, consistently, laps it all up for himself.

That same spirit who tempted someone within my home to rob my Pet Milk can bank is the same spirit who tempted me to steal and cheat in relationships and on exams over the years. God's Spirit encourages us to seek Him for His forgiveness. His forgiveness says that He will never remember our sins again! The **Lesson** that I learned was twofold. **Trusting includes knowing the importance of being discerning in our relationships with people.** I have learned that "the heart in man is deceitful above all things and beyond cure; who can know it?" (Jeremiah 17:9). Each person (including myself) is tempted when by his own evil desire he is enticed. Desire for unearned and unlawful gain is the evil which entices our souls to yield to the love of money's temptation. The other part of the **Lesson** that I learned is that **the *tempter* doesn't discriminate**. Thieves and victims – we are all the same, in need of repentance and forgiveness. The final **Word of Truth** says:

*Do not judge and criticize and condemn others, so
that you may not be judged and criticized and
condemned yourselves. For just as you judge and
criticize and condemn others you will be judged
and criticized and condemned, and in accordance
with the measure you deal out to others it will be
dealt out again to you. Matthew 7:1-2, Amplified*

Repentance

Within MY depths – where my soul does
     mourn
alongside the *wailing* from past mental
     scorn
I long to *forgive – and forget* – what my
     heart does sentence
constantly awakening in me the thought
     of true **Repentance**

My deception to err in false forgiveness
     was subtle
sincere words, spoken in faith, in need of
     rebuttal
for my heart did hide its unforgotten pain
the fruit of social stereotyping for others
     to gain
Becoming a slave to unforgiveness, *evil*
     influenced my expression
limiting me to rewards according to the
     harm done by my regression
I will to confess to purify my heart
     through *Godly Repentance*
and to purge my soul's shadowing of my
     In Christ sentence

When what I want to say and do, I don't
  say and do, *all the time;*
and if what I repented from I continue to
  do – that's a crime!
Revealing the **Concealing** in the true
  state of my heart – *and the* –
Repealing of what **Godly Repentance**
  had done from my start
"As He is, so am I" – to this lost world –
  maturing in me – *and*
not the dog returning to what I had
  vomited, for the world to see
Oh, the agony of being the wretched and
  deceitful man that I am
living daily in ministry embracing this
  subtle and underproductive sham
Who will rescue me from this body of
  death's sentence, *framed?*
"Thanks be to God, through Jesus Christ,"
  is My Repentance named!

Every man and woman in ministry is
  faced with this satanic dilemma
Only a commitment to the faith of Christ
  removes this enigma
Examine who you think to be, and pray to
  find out who you *ain't*
**The Lord rebukes each one of us who is
  an *unrepentant saint***

Mom's instructions matured into **Lessons**
learned which benefited me daily as I encountered
cross-cultural environmental situations. Whether
family members or relatives or segregated or

integrated communities, I was trained to intro-spectively know what to do in any situation. The strength to say *I don't know* or just to say *No!* or to listen and hold my tongue as a conditioned reflex left me on occasion. Sometimes I yielded to pride and lust which produced behavior which led me down a path toward a great fall. I have experienced many in my life. But, because of Mom's teachings, I knew better and my conscience always reminded me of that fact. **Lessons** from Mom served as a correcting rod, tugging on the bit in my control tower, to encourage me back on the Way that benefited me and all those in my sphere of influence. She encouraged me that God had given me something special inside that could be of benefit to others. I could encourage people by working His gift out of me. In a *dysfunctional family*, which some professionals would label us to have been, children are required at a very young age to protect themselves against adults. I thank God that the **Lessons** that I learned from Mom before I was a teenager are the same **Lessons** that sustain my family and me even today. Jesus Christ was Mom's guiding Light and she passed what He taught her on to me. The instructional voice I hear is Christ Jesus – through my mom – passed on to me.

Upon meditating on Mom's **Lesson** to judge a person by the fruit in his life, I now look upon my father with mixed emotions. She taught me to "obey my parents in the Lord, for this is right and the first Commandment with a promise." Much of my life I had a challenge with the *"In the Lord"* part as most of the male role models in our family's environment did not habitually walk in the character of the Lord. Adults make excuses for relatives, especially parents. We tend to forgive whatever they do in error, honoring them in disobedience to God's Word, and yield to the pride in blood lines. God is not neutral about In Christness. Either a parent's actions are "In the Lord" or they aren't! Judgment of the standard of one's behavior is the Word of God.

My dad, as the self-ordained leader of our home, was not God's leader in our home. My mother steadfastly lived that role in spite of satan's attempt to sift her and stamp out God's purpose through her to our benefit. Evil's desire was for her to leave her children and expose them to the vultures and scavengers of this world. She offered up her life on the altar of service to God's family plan and purpose for my life, for she nurtured and protected and trained me up until such time as I could make informed decisions and take care of myself.

The intent of **Lessons** is to use the cumulative maturation of my experiences to inspire and encourage men, women and children to ask this question of each person in their lives: **"Do you wish me well?"** It is a truth-wringing question that every person must consider asking themselves and others. The responsibility of training up children to have God's purpose released through their lives is the mission of every Godly father and mother's conscience.

There were some important lessons that I did not learn at home. In athletics, the importance of preparation for combat was stressed emphatically. But not even Mom specifically rehearsed me in the importance of preparing to be a husband enough for the woman God would give me. The only counseling on marriage that I remember occurred when I was a senior in college. A class-mate of my first wife said to me about her, "She is a very fine Christian woman who is *good stock* to bear you many healthy sons." More than anything else, his statement impacted my choice of her to be my wife. That very callous remark from this man set in motion my *mental processing* of thinking about marriage. What I was to hear many years later from a female university professor which would have dramatically impacted my initial *mental processing* about marriage was, "Willie, do you think you will ever be man enough for one woman?" That is the question for all men to answer *before* they get married. My final judgment here is that my mother was woman enough for one man. Unfortunately for her, my father wasn't man enough for one woman. Lust was the blinding, driving force in my youth. Most if not all young men and women I knew were in need of training in pulling in the reins of their minds to be instructed to patiently await God's pointing to that special woman or man. Marriage in the steadfastness of the Spirit who filled my dear mom is the model to be passed on as valuable. Being man enough for one woman is being prepared to love and fulfill God's purpose in marriage to His woman who stands ready as woman enough for one man.

I labored young for my money
I worked earnestly to catch me some fame
But through it all . . .

Is True Forgiveness Forgetting?

Lesson: Only through Love is Forgiveness. As she blended back into our daily lives, Mom's love invaded my silence and resolve to be mentally isolated from my father, brothers and sister. We communicated better in that I melted into more than one word answers in response to her love-centered questions about what was going on in my life. I shared with her that an older boy in the neighborhood had worked on the docks unloading merchandise from all over the world. He said that his uncle, a Longshoreman, had encouraged him to invite me to the Union Hall in Wilmington, California. He thought I looked old enough to get by the screening and was strong enough to do the work required. Mom gave me her blessing and advised me to take care of myself and not try to do anything beyond my capacity. "You're still a very young man, William, so be careful working with all those *grown men!*" I liked it that she called me a *young man* and not a "boy."

My first day of pursuing work went like clockwork. My friend and his uncle picked me up at the bottom of the hill at around 6:30 a.m., drove us to Wilmington and dropped us off at the Union Hall. He instructed me to get a number – a "pea" – which placed me in a chronological order to be called out for work *after* the Union members had all been sent out on jobs. I was taller than most of the men there so I made myself less conspicuous by sitting in a corner. When my number was called, loud and clear – TWENTY-FIVE! – I leaped up and hurried to the window. The gentleman took my #25 "pea," never asked my age, and said, "Fill this paper out and bring it right back." I did and he gave me a slip containing information about where I was to report. As I was walking out the door, a total stranger asked me, "Do you need a ride? I think we're going to the same location." I thanked him and noticed for the first time that my main man was off to a different work location. I was on my own.

When we arrived at the job location there was a group of men assembled around a guy who stood on a platform passing out work assignments. After most of the men left in the direction of his pointing, he looked in my direction and extended his hand to receive my slip. Following his directional nod, I quickly jogged over to the location where I would spend the next eight hours and many hours during the weeks to come.

Standing beside a cargo ship I got a completely different perspective than I had from the side of the hill in Western Terrace. Now, I also knew what was inside these large ships, at least this one that I was to assist in unloading. It was bananas – by the stalk – and with the biggest tarantulas ever seen. That first day, as I stood at the end of a conveyor belt between rows of fifteen box cars on either side, I thought to myself, *Bring it on; I can do this.* The sight of the first stalks emerging in the distance out of the belly of that huge ship was a mesmerizing experience. A few moments later, those first stalks were coming fast upon us. I suddenly realized what my partner and I were supposed to accomplish: Take   the banana stalks off the belt and stack them neatly inside the box cars. We were supposed to take off the first and every fifteenth stalk thereafter – AND – *whatever else was left on the belt.* If we didn't pull them, they fell off the end of the belt onto the railroad tracks.

The first hour was a breeze. Then two guys up the line took a bathroom break and two more went to get water. Suddenly I knew why no one wanted the last station. I was pulling these seventy- to ninety-pound stalks of bananas as fast as I could, piling them on the dock before they ended up down on the tracks. In desperation, I pressed the emergency stop button in a survival mode. The red lights flashed and the sirens blared over our heads, pointing us out as the two guys who couldn't keep up with the flow. The supervisor's loud Southern voice roared, "Come on, young blood, you gotta keep up!" I rushed the six to ten stalks into the box car and apologized to the "boss man" as I pushed the button to resume the flow of "nannas."

By the end of the day I was exhausted and hungry because I hadn't brought lunch and had no money to buy food. Then I realized I had to walk the seven to eight miles home. When I got to the top of the hill and saw my mother standing there smiling, my heart leaped inside as she asked, "Aren't you hungry? You forgot your lunch." I said, "Yes, Mama, I did and I'm real hungry." She looked up at my face, asking how my first day on the docks had been. I'm sure she felt my muscles twitching as we went up the sidewalk and into our home. "Wash up. I've got a surprise for you." Minutes later she placed before me a huge plate full of spaghetti and meat sauce. I had done a man's day of work and I

After thirteen years
I was comfortable with the fears
Poker faced – not to be revealed
Strength is in what my face concealed!

Willie

Age 13 years
San Pedro, California

needed a man's portion of food.

The **Lesson** I learned that first day on the banana detail was that it is very important to do my share of work. It was a man's world of hard labor and I felt really good about myself as I vacuumed down the spaghetti and garlic toast my mom had saved for me. Mom asked me questions about my day and the men I had met and what impressions I had formed. No one else seemed to care. After showering I began organizing for the next day when I noticed by my bed a reminder that our baseball team had a championship game in a few days. Before falling asleep that night I asked my mom to awaken me early so I could walk the distance to the Union Hall and be on time to get my "pea."

The next morning my feet hit the floor as soon as Mama's hand touched my shoulder. I was washed up, had eaten a large bowl of oatmeal with three pieces of toast and was out the door in fifteen minutes, on my way to pull me some more bananas off that belt. When I got on the main highway en route, a truck stopped ahead and waited. I recognized the head out the window as one of the men I had worked with the day before. "You want a ride, young blood?" I jumped on the back of the truck and smiled as the morning wind whistled across my face. I thought it was really good to be alive here in California and have comfort that these White men up front driving were not taking me to a lynch mob. I thanked them as we walked from their parked truck into the hall.

I got only a few days of work during the next several weeks but the checks I received for the days I'd worked were very encouraging. My baseball coach appeared happy to see me at the park practicing on the days I didn't get work and I still kept my lawn business customers satisfied. The coach said, "Naulls, the big game is a few days away and you haven't been consistently at practice. Will you be ready?" "Yes, sir! I am ready."

It seems not so long ago that I was 13 years old and living in that low-income housing project in San Pedro, California. As a developing young athlete, my daily life consisted of doing my chores, studying for school, working to make me some money, getting enough food and playing sports. Our housing project baseball team, without uniforms and equipment, advanced to the Southern California championship game that was to be played in Torrance. It is difficult to describe in words how excited I was, as this championship was like the World Series to me. We had no TV in my home; but every day during the baseball season, I listened to "recreated" professional games done by an announcer named Hal Berger on the radio. The Dodgers of Brooklyn, Yankees of New York City, Red Sox, Cardinals, Tigers, Reds, etc., were right there in my bedroom with me, and every pitch was delivered to *me* at bat. My mind exploded with possibilities as this announcer took me on trips to cities and ball parks that I thought were in another world, on another planet. I read books in school and did reports on the legends of baseball. There were no major league professional sports teams in southern California during my youth. The stories of legendary baseball players' lives became my hope to get out of the hell hole of my dad's rule and do something with my life. I was driven and motivated to some day be there, at bat, and on the pitcher's mound, in professional baseball.

The young men on our *project's* team represented the rainbow coalition of minority racial groups from around the world. Families had sped to San Pedro, California, from the Philippines, Yugoslavia, Italy, South and Central America, Mexico, and even as far away as China. Most of the parents of the starters on our team had migrated from the South, as my family had, and we were very aware of the new sense of freedom that we experienced in San Pedro. Living next to each other we daily had open communication with people of all skin colors for the first time in our lives.

This background information is to shed some light on the magnitude of this inter-community, inter-sectional baseball game between the district undefeated winner of the *have-nots* and the winner of the *haves*. Our opponent was a well-oiled, well-trained, disciplined baseball organization which had as much money, training, coaching, equipment, uniforms, and community support as any team has ever had or needed in the history of youth amateur sports. The biggest problem for our opponent was to hold back the laughter when they saw us showing up, one by one, sometimes two or three together. We had to walk from San Pedro to the game site which was several miles away as most, if not all, of our parents were at work.

What I remember vividly from that scene was the look of over-confidence in the eyes of our opponents. Their superiority complexes manifested into condescending laughter and remarks which demonstrated their disdain toward us have-nots. And, as we began this historical encounter, the opposition's coach yelled at me, as I stood on the pitcher's mound, poised to make the first pitch of the game. "Hey you, Willie, you big ugly NIGGER! You look like a clown out there, all of you. No uniforms. You are a disgrace to baseball and you should be in a zoo with the rest of the animals." His young players *and their parents* all laughed, and some even echoed this man's hostility. Even the umpire was amused as he smirked and shouted, "Play ball!" I fixed my eyes on this group of fellow humans and tuned out their hostile words as I studied their eyes. What I saw was fear and insecurity. Through the thought of rage and tears, I recorded every face on that team which spiritually imploded in opposition to itself. Even today that framed thought passes before me to forgive and forget. In response to their hostility, my sub-conscious control tower flicked on the switch to my mom's **Lessons. She raised up in me a conditioned reflex to go from any distracting frame to the next, which was my purpose – to get out the first batter standing at the plate.**

After the fifth inning of this seven-inning championship game, as I walked from the pitcher's mound, I glanced under the bib of my cap at that same group – whose hostile tactics had attempted to move me toward getting away from the task at hand, namely to win "the game." They now appeared dazed in disbelief, for not only had I struck out fourteen of the fifteen batters, but in addition I had dominated them with my own Louisville Slugger. When I sat down in the dugout, my mother's words came to me. She had often told me not to mirror evil but to be gracious in victory and defeat! But – also – to "never count the chickens before they hatch."

When the last batter swung and missed my final 90+ mph pitch in this championship game, he was the nineteenth batter of the twenty-one that I faced who turned away in disgust toward his dugout. Not one of their players reached first base, and the only two batters to hit the ball grounded out from third to first. The only perfect no run/no hit game of my baseball career. Final score: 7 to 0. My teammates mobbed me on the pitcher's mound, as the other team reluctantly came out in awe and apologized to me for the remarks they had made. The coach, through his cigarette-stained, wrinkled, discolored lips, said, "Willie, I was only trying to get you off your game so we could win." I didn't talk much in those days, so I just nodded with a tug on my cap and caught a frame as I towered over that group which had inflicted mental scars that bring tears to my eyes even as I write about it today.

I haven't forgotten, but have I forgiven? Yes, I have forgiven, but not forgotten. One of those opposing players, who became a medical doctor, I believe was my college basketball teammate at UCLA, but we never discussed "the game." I have often wondered what happened to all of those players, on both teams, and how the "givers" and "receivers" were affected by that evil spirit who used the opposing coach and players in "the game" to promote a separatist agenda that day. How were they affected by "the game"? I don't know. Did my teammates forgive and forget? Did the opposition forget? Did they learn anything by their very weak tactics? Were their *seeds* dried up and unproductive on the earth? For eternity? I never prayed that God would forgive them, for they knew not what they had done. But – I did forgive them and I have prayed to God and He has forgiven us all. Is forgiving – forgetting? Or does writing about this concept of forgiving to forget prove it to be an oxymoron? I think – spiritually, yes. Godly forgiveness is our standard. He never remembers our sins forgiven. With God, Forgiving is Forgetting.

The profound worldly **Lesson** that I learned was that **"you can't judge a book by its cover,"** which is interesting when you consider the Spiritual Lesson Christ taught: **You can tell what the tree is by its fruit. This spiritual concept is Truth in that one cannot know who the tree (the human) is until it (he or she) produces fruit from choices – seed plantings – made when participating in the games of our lives.**

"Get Dem Books"

"Get Dem Books!" My dad's consistent *walk by* gun-slinger one-liners. He came and went, in and out of my focusing. Kindergarten was the **Lesson** that started me on the path of learning how to prepare myself to communicate and compete. To read was to know what others have passed on to compare with what I thought about any subject. My father was convinced that "dem books" were the key to getting jobs and the more you knew, the better job you could get. My mother always put it another way. She said that I would be able to better take advantage of what some people call *luck* if I were prepared academically and spiritually for each opportunity God would present to me. She believed and taught that only God could break the *yoke* of hatred that White folk in Dallas, Texas, had contrived to control the destiny of her children.

So I believed from a very young age that teachers had the *mother lode* and I wanted to mine my share. In grammar school and junior high school I was a conscientious student who received "A's" and "B's" in most classes for my effort. The only "C" that really stands out in my mind was in junior high school for a lack of trying in gymnastics for half of a semester of physical education. Doing head-first tumbling was, for some reason, a stumbling block for me and my 6' 2", 7th grade mental development. By the end of the semester I received a "B" grade from Mr. Ruff, but only after he was made aware of the fact that the grade in his class determined whether or not I would be honored as a *Master*

Mariner, signifying achievement of a minimum 3.5 grade point average.

Richard Henry Dana Junior High School is located at 15th Street on Cabrillo Avenue. On the same street two blocks east was the San Pedro Boys Club. There is no way for me to overemphasize the importance of these two institutions in my life's development.

My seventh grade English teacher, Miss Woodard, taught us the rules of grammar and introduced us to poetry and the enjoyment of reading books. Each student was evaluated on his or her reports before the class, creative writing skills, and memorization and recitation of poetry. Charts were pinned on the wall just outside the classroom listing graphically each student's accomplishments before the entire school. My very competitive nature was awakened and fueled under her system of rewards. On a day near the end of the semester, she said, "Class, I want to share with you what I consider to be an extraordinary expression. Your assignment was to express yourself freely in verse and one of you has given a gift to all of us." She began to read, and I thought, *Wow, that's pretty good.* As she neared the end of the poem, she looked up and directly into my eyes with tears in her own as she said, "William, thank you. *You're on your way to openness of thought and expression. Don't deny the journey.*" I was surprised as I had not recognized the words which I had written. The emotions were new and confusing and embarrassing to me, but I liked the feeling of being recognized in open competition which did not judge me first as the only one of my skin color in the class. Unbiased evaluation of what I had to say creatively caused me to exhale a sigh.

My next breath inhaled hope of unimpeded growth.

Another gratifying class that I took in junior high school was Art Appreciation. Developing individual Christmas cards out of my own imagination was an experience I thoroughly enjoyed. I don't remember the teacher's face or name, only the encouragement of her kind words to continue to explore my creative self.

Mr. Kipling was my Social Studies teacher in the 7th grade and he honored me as his top student by assigning me to write and administer the final exam. I thought to myself, *This is good stuff here.* My head size doubled to keep my ego from oozing out of my ears. *I get to write the exam and know what the answers are to each of the questions I develop.* It suddenly occurred to me that there was a connection there that I hadn't considered. School wasn't about my getting a grade but was centered in my knowing and understanding the material presented. Mr. Kipling honored me and I was standing at the head of his class with a sea of my classmates' White faces glaring in astonishment. Central and South American countries, their people, cultures, history and location in the world were all consuming. My final exam to his class reflected my curiosity of minor locations of interest. The common remark was, "Naulls, I'm glad you don't make up the exams in all our classes." After my senior year of basketball at UCLA, I traveled to all of the places that were central to my exam questions there in the 7th grade. Of all the opponents of their college team which won two consecutive NCAA basketball championships, the University of San Francisco Dons chose me to be their guest on a two-month

Willie,
Bill Russell,
K. C. Jones and the
University of San
Francisco Dons
Basketball Team
arrive in Guatemala

16 June 1956

Fulfilling my
dreams from 7th
grade, we toured
Central and South
America, sponsored
by the U. S. State
Department.

United States State Department tour of South and Central America. God is Good. He gave me a mom who saw those things that be not as though they were. Her **Lesson**: "You will be able to better take advantage of what some people call luck if you are prepared academically and spiritually for each opportunity God presents to you" took on a new meaning.

That same semester back in junior high school, I played organized basketball as captain of my homeroom team. Something was released inside me. My body responded to my mind's desires to run and maneuver and execute toward winning with a purpose by the rules of engagement. It was as though unbroken horses had been pent up inside of me for the first years of my life and were now being trained to run using my muscles and lungs with my mind as director. Basketball, softball, handball, football and track were all day, every day, full time commitments of thought and action. I couldn't get enough and spent increasing amounts of time running and jumping and racing toward winning and being #1.

Physical Education was directed by my gym teachers at Dana. Retrospectively, they were the best. After all my subsequent years of experience, I believe that Mr. Briggs, Mr. Huff, Mr. Lynch and Mr. Ruff taught us *physical fitness* better than anyone since then. They instructed us and encouraged us to be involved in every sport. They laid the foundation of all physical fitness business of today, stressing cardiovascular endurance and muscular stretching and development. I excelled in basketball, softball, handball and football in after school league competition. As a 7th grader, I was encouraged by

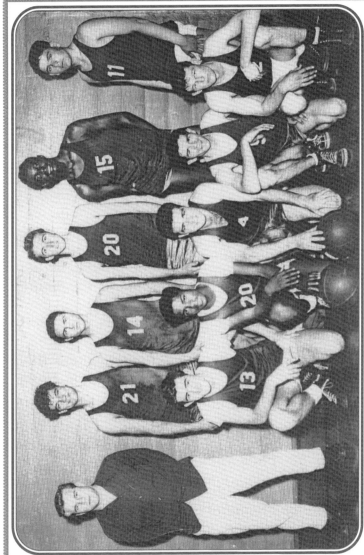

San Pedro Boys Club

Coach Mitch Vladimir and the *Southern California Championship Team*

Summer between my 9th & 10th Grade Years

the coaches to play with the 9th graders because they thought I would learn more. They encouraged me to not limit myself but to do my best against any opponent. From the 7th through the 9th grade, I developed into a very competitive young athlete as our teams from San Pedro traveled to other areas and were successful in winning most sectional competition.

Walking the many miles to school or riding my bike to and from the athletic facilities in and around San Pedro provided me with quality time to reflect on what was currently happening in my life. Almost every day after school I spent time at the San Pedro Boys Club. I know – it's now called the San Pedro Boys and Girls Club, but in my youth No Girls were allowed. Nick Trani, the Director, took a special interest in me and looked past my skin color and into the heart of the talent God had given me. He looked into the grace we shared, as I am convinced now that Nick was called to the priesthood of his Catholic conviction but never responded to that call. There were very few African American children who were members of the Club so that made me stand out, but he emphasized my uniqueness by hiring me to referee games and by giving me responsibilities to take care of the gym keys and supervise its use when he and Mitch were away on errands. Mitch Vladimir was the coach of our Club teams and we won every tournament we played in against other teams in the Southern California area.

After years of being away from San Pedro, I saw Nick Trani and we talked about his love for his wife and family and art. He discovered that God had given him a special gift to share with the world and

I'd love to sit down with every one of these faces and learn their lives' stories since this photo taken by Nick Trani.

San Pedro Boys Club Banquet

10th Grade

anything that God gives a man is good. I realized after our one-on-one session that I had leaned on him when I was young because he offered me his shoulder of kindness. We were Christian brothers, whether I realized it or not. My mother taught me to listen to hear whether or not someone wished me well. I heard and saw and benefited from Nick's trust in me. I knew that he wished me well. When I spoke at his memorial service at St. Anthony's Church, I shared with his family how honored I was to tell them all how much I loved Nick Trani – but – most significant to my life's development, he demonstrated God's love toward me.

As I drove from the service, I looked upon Cabrillo Avenue Grammar School, passed by the San Pedro Boys and Girls Club and then, two blocks further, Dana Junior High School. My heart was overjoyed with memories. The tears of joy overflowed as visions of those days in the trenches of life's development passed before me and I yelled from deep within whoever I am, *Thank you, Lord! Thank you, Mama! Thank you, Nick!*

Because of my emphasis on sports, the light which had been illuminated inside me in Miss Woodard's class was dimming from lack of fuel, but I didn't even notice. The rewards and awards came every season, and by the end of my senior year in high school I was recognized as one of America's best in basketball and baseball. It would be over fifteen years later before the bright light of fame in athletics would flicker enough for me to evaluate the reality of my myopic and limiting choices. Even now, several years past the last goal scored, I am often reminded by others of how successful I was in my job of being a collegiate All-American at UCLA, a four-year All-Star with the New York Knicks and three-time World Champion with the Boston Celtics during my ten year professional basketball career. These very physically competitive institutions exploited and used up what I could do in competition. Time of reflecting on the fruit of one's choices is vital for debriefing, for course-correcting and for impacting one's *next move*.

Miss Woodard had instructed me that I was more than the last goal scored. She had said all those many years ago, "Don't deny the journey . . . of openness of thought and expression." My pursuit of fame and fortune in sports blinded me to thoughts of the inner journey to self expression. However, the **Lessons** of my mom and, later on, my college coach, John Wooden, were stored deep in the recesses of my mind and a vision for life after sports began to take on form. **Lesson:** What you think to do is you. Your actions paint a picture of your character. What others say about you is your reputation. Mom taught me early to know: "William, God is in you to do of His good pleasure. . . . Work to become the best man He has created you to be."

Junior High School was a positive growth experience for me. By May of my ninth grade year I was ready to go up *on the hill*. San Pedro High School's baseball playing field, which doubled as its football practice field, was visible from below on Dana Junior High's black-topped athletic playing surfaces. It was about two blocks away with nothing in between except a five- to seven-story building height hillside terrain. The star pitcher on *our* Pirate team was Tom Lovrich. Near the end of baseball season all of us developing athletes scaled the hill to watch him pitch against phenom Paul Pettit of Narbonne High who became the first Major League $100,000 bonus baby. The game was awesome in retrospect. Pettit had the same fluid motion, power and build of the former Yankee and now Houston Rocket Andy Pettitte. Lovrich was a thinner version of the great Don Drysdale.

What an impression I was left with after that game. I said to myself, *I can do this.* Some of the players on both teams recognized me from competition in the various leagues around town. My self confidence surged and I sensed a mounting encouragement that I would succeed in high school. My ninth-grade friends Jay Wright and Charley Cline lived and died on every pitch until the Pirates made the last out in a losing effort. As we walked back down the hill Jay, my future baseball team-mate, said, "Willie, you are as good as those guys."

"We'll see next year, won't we," was my humble but confident response.

In preparation for my trip *up the hill*, I achieved several Number One accomplishments: the one wall handball championship, hop-step-and-jump (now triple jump) championship, over-the-line championship, and football, softball and basketball accuracy and distance throwing and performance supremacy. My friends and classmates were very successful in athletics in future years. The Johnson brothers – Lynn, Herb and Sammy Lee – were all of professional baseball caliber but never got a chance because the high school coach never opened up his program to them. Lynn is father to former Celtic great Dennis Johnson. (I remember Dennis's mom as the best female athlete at Dana Junior High

Grabbing a Rebound as a 10ᵗʰ Grade Starting Guard

All-City Cousin Mac is at the right evaluating his star pupil

School, followed closely by Saddis V. Hearn.) Herb
was an All-City fullback, but Lynn and Sam were
both discouraged and were limited to summer and
semi-pro heroics. Don Shinnick became an All-City,
All-American (UCLA) and All-Pro linebacker with
the Johnny Unitas Colts. Anthony Morich became a
star at Stanford University, Jim Decker a track and
football performer at the University of Southern
California, Roland Harvey an All-State high and low
hurdler champion, Louie Morales an All-City tight
end, Horace Davis an All-City caliber lineman,
Louie Medina an All-City center fielder in baseball,
and, of course, my cousin Mac, a two-time All-City
magician who laid the foundation of excellence
for all that would follow him in basketball. My
brother succumbed, as did many others of the few
Black athletes during my time, to the rejection of
their skin color by coaches and teachers.

My cousin, Million Harvest (M. H.) McGilvery,
was my basketball teacher and role model. He was
three years older and two grades ahead of me and
made the All-City team twice. We spent the entire
summer before my first year of high school practicing one-on-one on the courts of Gompers Junior
High School in south central Los Angeles. He
always beat me – every game. But I was learning
and the scores got closer and closer. Near the end of
that summer I noticed one day that I was looking
down into the eyes of my cousin. He was 6' 3 1/2"
tall and I had grown to 6' 5". I blocked more and
more of his shots and knew his every move. I
noticed also that I could out-jump him and out-
rebound him; but he was still the best, most intelligent shooter with the widest variety

of shots the City of Los Angeles had ever developed. *Maximilliano the Magician* was his name and basketball was his *fame*.

And then it happened: Nearing the end of a very close game, I blocked his left handed hook shot, took the ball behind the free throw line, as required by one-on-one rules, turned, raised up, squared off and fired for glory. Cousin Mac looked shell-shocked as the ball swished through the net. His young protégé cousin – for the first time – had just beat him one-on-one. He snarled, "Loser's ball." He took it out and was on offense, and it happened again. I won! And again, I won and won yet again until he said, "I've got to go home. We'll continue this later." He never beat me again because we never played one-on-one again.

Lessons I Learned from My Teachers, Coaches and Mentors

I was very excited when San Pedro High School basketball tryouts for the varsity and junior varsity teams began the autumn of my sophomore year. *Up on the hill*, overlooking our junior high school and the Pacific Ocean in the distance, Coach Bob Tabing pitted me against my cousin Mac during the first full court scrimmage and we were at it again. Cousin Mac actually stopped speaking to me because the competition was so real that color and kin folk were forgotten – *for real*. The only real deal in competitive sports is to win some playing time in games and to win it for times that count. So I battled against every one of the returning starting five: Nick Trutanich, 6 ' 5" guard; Mark Pesusich, 6' guard; Ben Hansen, 6' 6" forward; Bill Stevens 6 ' 6" forward; and cousin M. H. McGilvery, 6' 3 1/2" center.

After three weeks of intense practice and full court scrimmages, the coach called us together to inform us of his choice for the varsity and junior varsity teams, including the starting lineup for opening the season. He posted his choices on the gym wall and walked out. I was out the door on my way home without looking at the list when an African American football player caught me outside and said, "Man, Willie Naulls, Willie Naulls, you made the first string, man." Then another of my tenth grade classmates who made the junior varsity roster ran up and grabbed me, shouting, "Willie, you made the first string as a guard." My cousin came over and said, "Good work," and left to catch

San Pedro Pirates
Varsity Basketball
Starting Five
1950

Uncrowned City Champions

Forward **Benny Hansen** 6'6"
Forward **Bill Stevens** 6'6"
Center *Million Harvest (M. H.) McGilvery* 6'3 1/2"
Guard **Nick Trutanich** 6'5"
Guard **Willie Naulls** 6'6"

10th Grade

Globe-Trotter Willie

in the 10th Grade

the Red Car, for his family had moved out of San Pedro to the south central Los Angeles area, about 20 miles to the north. He commuted daily, as I did later during my final year of competition at San Pedro High.

Los Angeles didn't have a citywide basketball tournament during Mac's senior season but, had there been a tournament, I'm sure we would have won the city championship. We lost one practice game in overtime to University High School because Coach Tabing didn't let the first string play in the first half. He said we hadn't hustled in practice the previous few days. But that was the only blemish on our record. Nick and Cousin Mac made the first team All-City at guard and center, respectively, and Mac was clearly the outstanding player in the city. They, along with Ben and Bill, were the four on our team honored as first team All-League, Mac being named Most Valuable Player. I was honored on the second or third team All-League.

Baseball was clearly my best sport up to entering high school as I had already played and pitched against many older and professional players. When I went out for varsity, there were many familiar players trying out for both the varsity and junior varsity teams. On a day that Coach Tabing posted the names of those who had made the varsity team, I actually expected my name to be on that roster. In reality, in summer competition I had defeated each and every one of those players who tried out for the varsity. My name was not on the list and my new junior varsity coach was a very gentle man named Leonard Martin. He came up to me and put his hand on my shoulder. He assured me that I was good enough to play varsity but that the team was loaded with very good senior players (all White) and he promised me that I would get my chance. I was surprised by his compassion but disappointed, even when I was promoted to the varsity for the playoffs at the end of the season. I never pitched past warming up in the bull pen during our final losing effort in the City Championship game. As a junior varsity team, we were champions and my pitching and hitting were instrumental in our success.

That summer between my sophomore and junior years, a teammate acting as messenger brought me a request from his coach. I was asked to play with San Pedro's American Legion team. The coach had refused to look at me the year before and denied me a tryout because he didn't like the color of my skin. Many years later, after his death, I accepted an invitation to be a guest speaker when he was inducted into their Hall of Fame; but when I was young, he had already made my Hall of Shame. So when one of my schoolmates, who was on the previous year's American Legion team and who was on the second team of the high school's junior varsity baseball team, approached me, I said, "No," emphatically. He returned several times later, but my *No* meant *No*. His coach never spoke to me face to face because his pride couldn't tolerate asking my skin color to help build his reputation through winning. God has said that "pride comes before the fall."

After that summer, my junior basketball season rolled around and we were introduced to our new leader, Coach Bob Bell from somewhere in Utah. He

San Pedro Pirates Baseball Team
1951 Los Angeles City Finalists

Coach Leonard Martin was a very gentle and kind spirit.
He encouraged all of us to do our best.

I pitched and won four straight games in the Los Angeles City Tournament.
Rules prohibited me from pitching in the Championship game.

Top Row: Coach Leonard Martin, Perry Carter, Lou Medina, Louie Bogdonovich, Jay Wright, "Grits" Iacono, Walter Brown

Bottom Row: Ray Locke, Randy Lewis, Willie Naulls, Robert Kirkland, Jack Lovrich, Martin Zuanich, Felix Meraz

11th Grade

was a tall, wiry, no-nonsense man who wanted to establish his authority. He pushed me and made me a better rebounder by digging his bony and space-demanding elbows into my ribs. He taught me to take space on the court rather than waiting to see if it were occupied. About mid-season I twisted my ankle severely in a game and missed several games, returning just in time for the city championship tournament. We ended up losing in the first round of the tournament that year and I believed along with my coach that we could have won it all if I had been at least 75% healed of my ankle injury. At the close of our season, at the awards banquet, in a stern voice looking into my eyes, Coach Bell said, "Next year will be our year, right, Naulls?" I looked him straight away and shouted, "Right, Coach!"

After all my commitments to basketball were honored, I was reminded by one of my baseball teammates from the year before that tryouts had already happened and my name was already posted on the varsity roster. He added, "There is also a new varsity coach, Coach Leonard Martin." Coach Martin had long expressed confidence in me and my ability during my sophomore year and encouraged me to take my time to get into shape. Our team had a near perfect season, losing again in the final city-wide championship game. Because of Los Angeles City high school tournament rules, a pitcher couldn't pitch two games in one day, so although I won four games in a row to get us into the finals, I was barred from pitching in the final game. I was honored to be on the first team All-City as a pitcher. Coach Martin was very happy for me.

I controlled my own destiny when I was on the mound pitching. I know it takes a team to win; but I thought that if I struck out every batter, they would have to play me.

When I stood on the pitcher's mound, I thought "I AM THE KING"

Willie

11th Grade

NO. 2 FOR 'WALLOPIN' WILLIE — Willie Naulls, San Pedro High pitcher, touches the plate after his second home run against Jordan yesterday. Coach Leonard Martin compris the welcoming committee. The catcher is J dan's Earl Battey.

Pirate Fans 15, Homers Twice

No. 2 FOR 'WALLOPIN' WILLIE

Willie Naulls, San Pedro High pitcher, touches the base after his second home run against Jordan [High School] yesterday. Coach Leonard Martin comprises the welcoming committee. The catcher is Jordan's Earl Battey.

Naulls' 15 strikeouts ran his season total to 49 in 32 1/3 innings. The seven shutout frames lowered his earned run average to a neat .195.

11th Grade

Medina and Naulls Named on All-City Baseball 1st Team

By MIL CHIPP
News-Pilot Sports Editor

Courtesy of San Pedro News-Pilot

Pitcher Willie Naulls and Outfielder Lou Medina, who doubles in brass as the San Pedro High student body president, today were named to the All-Los Angeles City prep baseball team for 1951. Both were unanimous choices for the mythical team. . . .

A 6'5" junior, Naulls turned in an excellent 12-2 season record this campaign for one of the best over-all marks in the city. Named "Player of the Year" in the Eastern-Marine circuit, Naulls whiffed 75 batters during regular loop competition. His strikeout total for the entire season, including exhibition tilts, was near the 150 mark. . . . .

(Future Hall of Fame Manager of the Cincinnati Reds George (Sparky) Anderson, then junior short-stop for Dorsey High School, was also named to this All-City Team.)

BREAKING ALL SCHOOL SCORING AND REBOUNDING RECORDS

Courtesy of San Pedro News-Pilot

*I am the conductor of this shot
and the three defenders are in concert*
12th Grade

NAULLS' 49 POINTS AGAINST GATORS WINS CITY SCORING TITLE

Courtesy of San Pedro News-Pilot

Pirate Cage Ace Averages 28.1 Per Game; Sets Record

The 6'6" Pirate center, with the reach to match, yesterday scored 49 points to better his own school record and come within a whisker of establishing two new city marks . . . .

12th Grade

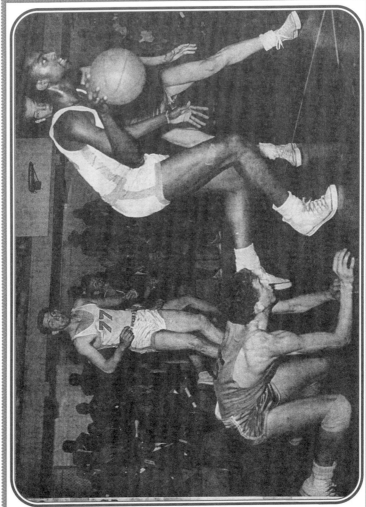

*Pushing on toward
the prize in a*
City
Championship
Semi-Final Game
against
University High
School

*Denny Miller,
Gorton's Fish's man,
is guarding me and
my teammate
Billy Jackson
is in the background*

12th Grade

When my senior basketball season began in the fall of my last year at San Pedro High School, I had already made All-City in baseball and basketball during my junior year. Coach Bell welcomed us with a high degree of expectation and we lived up to his standard and won the City Championship. I led the city in scoring and rebounding, averaging 28.1 points and 16.7 rebounds per game. Along with future major league baseball player Earl Battey, I was Los Angeles City Co-Player of the Year for the 1951-52 basketball season. We had split the two games against his all Black high school team during the regular season. They lost in the semi-finals of the city tournament to a team of all minority players that we beat to win the championship. There was one other African American player that started for us that year, Sam Johnson, who was very quick at guard. He made the All-League first team.

This two-year span was the most demanding of my high school days. Academic school work became less and less of a priority and I spent very little time thinking in depth about what I was supposed to be learning for future use. I thought only about getting by – just staying eligible and completing all of my required college prep courses. Athletic excellence demands one's *prime time*. UCLA and Coach Wooden were the choice of most of the All-City basketball first team selections, but Battey eventually opted for professional baseball. Morris Taft and Denny Miller ("Gorton's Fisherman") came to UCLA with me. Barry Brown from Venice High School went on to become a prominent arch rival at Stanford University.

NAULLS SCORES 34 – BUCKETS
THIS ONE-HANDER WITH EASE

MIRRORFOTO–Courtesy of *The Mirror*

Two University High School defenders appear to be doing a graceful dance as they try in vain to stop San Pedro's Willie Naulls from scoring in the City Tournament Semi-Final Game.

12th Grade

NAULLS SCORES 22
AS PIRATES ANNEX CROWN

Willie Naulls of San Pedro reaches for rebound and tosses it back into hoop for field goal in the Los Angeles City Championship Final Game against the Polytechnic Mechanics.

12ᵗʰ Grade

San Pedro Pirates Varsity Basketball Team

Los Angeles City Champions
1952

Coach Bell taught us well. I commuted daily over 50 miles round-trip from Watts to San Pedro to finish my high school experience with these guys. None of them, even Coach Bell, knew how much each of them meant to me. We did lay it on the line every game. Thank you, Mrs. Bell, for the wonderful steak dinners you made for me during our Championship run.

Top Row: Manager Walter Brown, Clarence "Goose" Gravett, John Zlatic, Fred Sherseth, Nick Zorotovich, Mose Harris, Danny Solaro, Coach Bob Bell

Bottom Row: Wayne Osborne, Marion "Germ" Podue, Billy Jackson, Sam Johnson, Willie Naulls, Stan Kobsef, Joe Mardesich, Vince "Gopher" Flamengo

12ᵗʰ Grade

NAULLS, BATTEY HEAD ALL-CITY PREP HOOPMEN

PLAYERS OF THE YEAR

Earl Battey, Jordan, Forward   William Naulls, San Pedro, Center

Los Angeles Times photo

Barry Brown, Venice, Forward   Morris Taft, Polytechnic, Guard   Denny Miller, University, Guard

Naulls, first Pirate ever honored as cage Player of the Year,
led Bob Bell's bucketeering Buccaneers to the first city championship
snared in any competition by the portside institution.

Earl Battey and I were the only Blacks on the first team Los Angeles All-City Baseball Team, as catcher and pitcher, respectively, during my junior year. We both were underclassmen with eligibility left. I mention this because that was my last baseball campaign in institutional organized competition. I really looked forward to my senior year's challenge after having come so close to winning it all, losing in the final championship game for two years in a row.

Spring baseball practice was in full bloom when I fulfilled my last commitment to basketball at the awards banquet. As I jogged out toward the practice field, adjusting my uniform in place, I noticed that my name was *not posted* on the recycled baseball Coach Bob Tabing's varsity roster. He had returned to coach baseball from wherever he had gone on sabbatical my junior year. Where was Mr. Martin? I reported to practice two days late because I had appeared at many school-sanctioned basketball award activities including trips to university campuses to evaluate and decide where I would accept a college scholarship. I was a little tired after returning from a visit to the University of California campus at Berkeley as I approached our team's meeting to continue my pursuit of excellence in baseball.

The coach was surrounded by the team as I walked up and, without hesitation at the sight of me, he yelled, "You may have been all-everything in basketball and even in baseball in previous years, but you're going to have to earn your way on this team." My mother's words emerged: "Be slow to speak and don't get angry." I said nothing. His stare was long as the saliva dripped from the side of

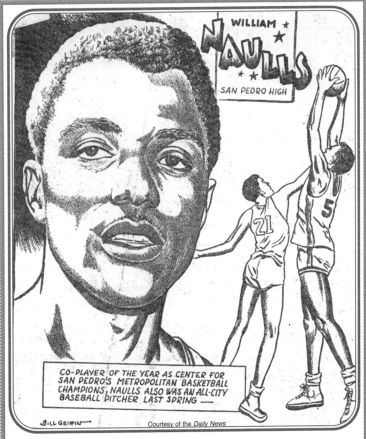

WILLIAM ★ NAULLS
SAN PEDRO HIGH

CO-PLAYER OF THE YEAR AS CENTER FOR
SAN PEDRO'S METROPOLITAN BASKETBALL
CHAMPIONS, NAULLS ALSO WAS AN ALL-CITY
BASEBALL PITCHER LAST SPRING —

BILL GRIFFIN→   Courtesy of the *Daily News*

High School Hall of Fame

By MORY KAPP

Only two athletes of Los Angeles mintage have ever made All-City first teams in two sports. One of these rare birds is San Pedro's mild-mannered, gold-bannered William Naulls, whose flights of fancy performance as basketball center and baseball pitcher bring him winging into the Daily News Hall of Fame. Naulls was not alone tabbed in a brace of pastimes – he was thrice robed with extra honors. In basketball the 17-year-old tip-in, lay-up, defensive rebound rampager led Bob Bell's charges to San Pedro's first city championship of any kind and he was fittingly eulogized as co-Player of the Year on Eastern-Marine and All-City combos.

Appropriately middle-monickered Dean after the illustrious Dizzy Dean of dazzling diamond renown, William Dean Naulls has been twirling out statistics that twinkle with ample justice to the immortal horsehide name.

As an unbeaten sophomore he won 10 games for Martin's loop kings; last season as varsity mainspring he clicked with 13 victories against two losses, including four low-hit shutouts and four historic successes in the Dorsey tournament.

Speed-unsparing Naulls, extremely agile for his height and gifted with exceptional control as he stretches his elongated cannon's mouth almost under the chin of the batter, fanned 75 bewildered clubbers in 52 Eastern-Marine innings, struck out 43 more in 28 tourney frames. He right-armed San Pedro through all of its triumphs to match the record unfurled the year before by Dorsey's headlining Ed Palmquist.

During the summer the tall Naulls was slinger for the Watts Giants. And who should be his battery mate but his fellow All-City Player of the Year, the versatile Earl Battey of Jordan, Naulls' stoutest through friendliest interscholastic rival.

On the hill an atom bomb could explode, says tutor Martin, and Naulls would remain as calm and unruffled as June lake in June. Only the batsmen get the "willies" as Willie keeps on top of 'em, as they go down blanked and blinking.

Fresh in the minds of maplewood fans is William's equally memorable exploits on the court where this rippler of the cords left his calling card with killing coolness and the following uncommon figures:

A 28.1 loop average, second only to the 28.9 city classic and crumpling the E-M standard of 22.2 constructed so laboriously only two years ago by none other than William's cousin, Million Harvest (the silvery) McGilvery, with whom William earned a hoop block as a sophomore guard on Bob Tabing's clean-sweeping E-M monarchs...

A hot 96 digits in the city tournament that evaporated the former four-game score of 94 ...

The tourney high of 34 points in a single game, the season's high of 50, only three off the metropolitan apex ...

Four times in the 12 loop outings Naulls, whose jump shot was all but unguardable, melted the pail with 35 points or more, twice reaching at least 40 ...

His accuracy both in field goal and free throw tries was notable as he arched eight charity tosses out of nine.

In his last year at Dana Junior High, William was a member of the Commodores, an honor society equivalent to the senior high school Knights, to which organization he has just been nominated.

His admirers, who esteem their hero with justified pride, anticipate another even louder-booming season for him in the coming baseball wars. When you praise his demonstrations of prowess they simply nod and say with deliberate but expressive distortion of grammar:

"You ain't seen nothin' yet. Wait'll you see William in the spring."

his twisted mouth. He spat and snorted, "You got to earn your way on my team."

Lesson: Mom often said, "When evil gains influence over a man, leave him be and pray for him. If he persists, have nothing to do with him."

After pitching and winning a few games, Coach Tabing finally pushed the last inch out of my tolerance. After yet another demeaning barrage of verbal attacks on me, I said before the entire team on my way off the practice field, "Coach, I can't please you." I hadn't changed, but he hadn't either. Could it be that my All-City year while he was away stirred in him a resentment that the sport was better off without him? I was in better shape than anyone on the team. My attitude hadn't changed. My mouth was always slow to speak, my ears were quick to listen and I never displayed the anger toward him which my heart entertained. What did I do or could I have done differently? I was raised to be obedient to authority given to coaches. I respected Coach Tabing's authority and yielded to him and did my best all the time. Again, I lived the ideal player image, being a respectful observer of the authority vested in teachers and coaches. So what was it that had this man's pride boiling over toward me? As I walked off the field toward my locker, he yelled in scorn, "You quitter! Look back here at all of your teammates that you are letting down." The words were like darts into the back of my soul but I did not turn around and confront him.

Counter Punch

How do you react when you're hit real
    hard?
like in the nose – causing that stuff to
    ooze out like lard?

You know what I'm saying?

An onslaught of the severest intensity
causing your mind to be captive of evil's
    propensity
Do you **Counter Punch** in like kind
    retort?
or can you restrain toward a peaceful
    resort?
Attacks are less often physical than one
    might suspect
so the discernment in God's Word your
    defense must direct
The devil is relentless – after your faith –
    to persist
over whom we have the victory in
    CHRIST JESUS to resist
A **Counter Punch** is effective when **"It is
    written"** is used
God's Word to the rescue, your attackers
    are defused!

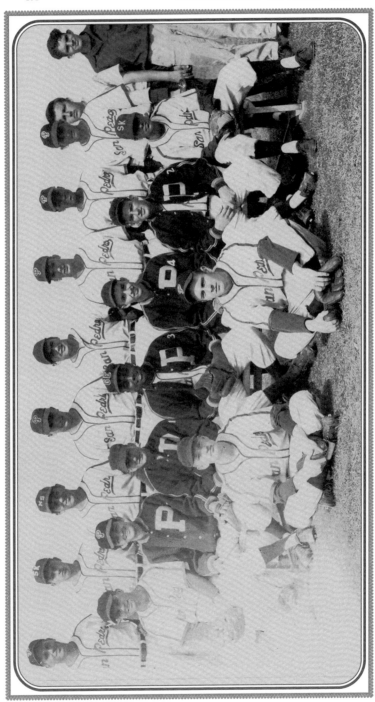

San Pedro Pirates Varsity Baseball Team
1952

I never played organized baseball after "quitting" this group of young men. What have their lives been since this day?

They voted me team captain for the second straight year, so I surely agonized over my decision to not share in their battles against the foes of the San Pedro Pirates.

Top Row: Coach Bob Tabing, Lou Bogdonovich, —, Maynard, Don Shinnick, Randy Lewis, Jay Wright, —, —, Manager Walter Brown

Middle Row: —, John Guardado, —, Willie Naulls, Martin Zuanich, —, Victor Hietala

Bottom Row: —, —

Others in this photo whom I don't recognize are Bob Chagnovich, Arlen LeVeir, Bob Ortega, Ronnie Pesusich, Anthony Tipich, and boys with the last names of Mercer and Thomas

12ᵗʰ Grade

In the locker room, after showering and dressing, some of my teammates shook my hand and asked how I had taken his abuse for so long. They also asked me to forget about him and come back because *the team needed me.* "We can win it all, Naulls, if you'll just come back and endure . . . ." I looked at their faces, realizing that they could never know what I feel or who I am. I thought, *How fortunate these White boys are to have coaches and leagues and cities pulling for them to replace me, no matter what the level of their talent.*

I just nodded and eased on out of the locker room to an area outside where, weeks before, this same coach had called one of my basketball teammates, Sam Johnson, a "nigger black box." He had physically assaulted Sam, taking sides with Big Marco who had instigated the confrontation, calling Sam a *Nigger.* Coach didn't care to hear the real story but only acted to protect the skin color matching his – that of the aggressor and *bully Marco* – against the smaller Sam. Sam had simply retaliated in fury of his soul against an attack. "Enough is enough," Sam screamed. "This White boy called me a name and hit me first. Enough is enough. I'm not taking that any more and I don't care what you do to me, Coach."

As mentioned above, Sam was first team All-League on our championship varsity basketball team led by Coach Bell. He was also an outstanding baseball player, as were many other African American players at San Pedro High School during my time there. They were never given a chance to exhibit their talent because the team had a White filter for a coach.

Tangled Web

Oh, what a tangled web is weaved
when skin color is used by those
    deceived
to play with lives, as one does chess
controlling ability's expression, but
    God is just
"Judge ye not," comes to the fore
God knows intent from within our
    core
Give it up, your decision to His care
those prone to evil, His wrath to
    bear

My mom was concerned for me when I didn't finish my high school course in the sport I loved and had the most talent in, baseball. That coach *intruded* beyond the limits of my tolerance at that time and place. Hindsight is speculatively 20-20 and I have often asked myself, "What if?" That question to myself came during and after all those many years of collegiate and professional glory in basketball had subsided. "Who cares?" Well, life is not a rehearsal, *but* my journey to *record*. And maybe, just maybe, my **Lessons** may be used by others for their *reward*. The coach's **intrusion** into the developing man in me was his visual illusion trying to introduce a spiritual contusion *in me*. I spat him out as foul and not for my future generations to dread.

Intrusion

Intrusion
is an invasion with the intent to
    spread
a doctrine for my future generations
    to dread
false superiority to plant in my head
skin deep identity of even the dead

Intrusion
perpetuating a visual illusion
introducing a spiritual contusion
spawning a satanic delusion
How damaging can be an Invading
Intrusion

Many, many years later that same coach, in his
final will and testament, asked his wife to request of
me that I, a Christian pastor, speak at his memorial
service. I had only seen him twice since high school
and we were cordial but distant. The first time was
in the middle of my professional basketball career.
My summer employment was as supervisor of
summer camps for the Los Angeles Department of
Parks and Recreation. I recognized a name which
appeared on a list of coaches to be considered
as clinic instructors – Bob Tabing. When he came in
for an interview, one of the questions asked by
evaluating board members was, Can you, in an
unbiased way, work with and under people of all
races and religions? He said he could. Some of the
other members detected a dryness and hesitation in

his answer. He was not selected, not because of his answer, but because of the enthusiastic response to that questions by other coaches who, later that summer, did a marvelous job for us with the kids of all racial and ethnic backgrounds. The next time I saw the coach was years after my retirement from professional basketball. I was asked to emcee a banquet in San Pedro. Before the banquet, we each offered a cordial hello. He then leaned over and whispered in my ear, "Do you want me to take over for you as emcee? Or if you need me to speak something, I will – for you." I stared at him again, all those years later, and told him firmly, "I think I can handle it, Coach!"

At the memorial service for Coach Bob Tabing, my Mom's words sprang up in me for the umpteenth time since agreeing to pay my last respects to one of my early teachers. **Lesson**: "If you don't have anything good to say about someone, don't say anything at all." So I spoke, sharing that he had made me a first team basketball player in my sophomore year of high school, which encouraged me. Consequently, I began my career there in confidence and hope for my future. What I didn't say was that some of his actions had forced me to make tough decisions which meant giving up my first love in sports, baseball. Foregoing the competition and pursuit of a city championship, the awards and glory and the prestige of finishing my senior year experience as a two-time All-City player in baseball left a hole in me. **I gave up a pursuit in professional baseball, my life long dream.**

Not playing tore at me inside and I never played baseball again in high school or college. It wasn't Coach Tabing's fault. It was my decision alone to walk off the field and away from baseball. MY PRIDE! A White player would never have had to make that decision, but I responded as an African American who thought that the coach had his racist foot firmly on the back of my neck. I was suffocating and it was within my power to fling him off like swatting a fly. He needed my talent to enhance his reputation more than I needed to regress back to hanging on to the belly of that dog called racism. No player in the history of the Los Angeles City Schools' Athletic Association had ever been All-City for two years in two sports. I could have been the first and the last. I believe I remain one of only two high school athletes in history to have made first-team All-City in two sports. What does it matter? It's just another story in the life of a man who, as a youth, was not allowed to express himself in open competition freely. The authority was unduly influenced by skin color first – and – last. How many African American athletes across the country could tell similar stories?

Mom's **Lesson**: "The world is not fair, son, but God is just." Dramatically influenced by that experience with Coach Tabing, I quit the game, thinking, *I'm more than a game.*

Lesson: "Let not many of [us] become teachers, knowing that we shall receive a stricter judgment" (James 3:1). **"Forgive to cleanse the way for God's judgment."** My Mom always taught that God is our final judge. Maybe – just maybe – God, through Coach Tabing, wanted to give me yet another chance to forgive – to forget that imprint of past hurts which settled in indelible ink of evil in my heart. That day, as I stood speaking to the full room of those assembled, I shared from my heart

my reaction to the positive memories about Coach
Tabing and responded to the positive things his life
long friends had to say about him. In an audio tape
recording made by him before his death specifically
to be aired at his memorial service, he mentioned
my name prominently, speaking as a voice from
the dead, promoting peace, which only God
administers to those who seek Him. My soul was
cleansed that day as my heart regurgitated the
hatred I had harbored all those years about my
high school senior year baseball disappointment.

Lesson: When I was called to ministry, my
epiphany with God commanded me to share "what
great things He had done in my life." Here is yet
another example of God's grace to give me more
insight into the importance of forgiveness.
Unforgiveness can be a burden unto the grave. It
would have been better for both Coach Tabing and
me if I had communicated with him before his
death. Apparently, by his appeal that I speak at his
memorial service, he was more of a Godly man than
I. God's Word taught me by my mom says:

> *"And when you stand praying, if you hold anything
> against anyone, forgive him, so that your Father
> [God] in heaven may forgive you your sins."*
> *Mark 11:25*

I pray that sharing this episode of my life will
inspire you to relieve yourself of unforgiveness.
Call whoever is a personality to whom you have
enslaved yourself through unforgiveness. Forgive
them, so that God in heaven may forgive you your
sins.

When the Going Gets Tough . . . .

In the EYE of the hearts of those who
    care,
and through their confession they might
    dare
to get going, when pressure to be
is not so popular for their group to see
And over the course of Faith's literacy
    test,
when given the chance to be God's best,
only through decision can in performance
    we view
what comes forth in the clutch that our
    hearts foreknew

Hidden behind the fear cloaked in
    expression
is a duplicity of voice of inner complex-
    ion
"Judgment is mine," said our Lord so
    clear,
learn of Me for your cross to bear
When the going gets tough, take the
    route I point;
Get to going in the Peace of the Way I
    anoint

My accomplishments through high school include:

Academic Achievements:

Dana Junior High School:

Master Mariner, Commodores Honor Society

San Pedro High School *Knights* Honor Society

Daily News High School Hall of Fame

Athletic Achievements:

Baseball Honors:

Western Terrace Project Team: Pitched perfect no-run, no-hit, shutout in Southern California Championship

Southern California Youth MVP

San Pedro High School:

Junior Varsity: Captain; Pitched to a record of 10-0 in unbeaten season

Team Championship

Varsity: Captain two years

Pitched to a record of 13-2 in junior year

League MVP, junior year

Los Angeles All-City, junior year

Los Angeles City Finalist, two years

Basketball Honors:

San Pedro Boys Club:

Southern California Championship

San Pedro High School:

Varsity three years; Captain two years

All-City two years

Career School Records in Scoring and Rebounding

Led City in Scoring and Rebounding, senior year

Los Angeles City Championship, senior year

Los Angeles Co-Player of the Year, senior year

Levitating . . . .

Academics became less and less important to me as I spent my quality time in preparation for athletic competition and glory. I do remember giving my all in the final stretch of a Spanish class taught by Miss Vega. Spanish was a very easy and beautiful language to learn and I just did not put the time in until I decided that I wanted to get an "A" in Spanish on my transcript. The final exam was composed of two sections: verb conjugations and sentence structure and word usage. It was an exhaustive exam requiring students to know everything taught during the year. Well, I absolutely aced the exam. The only red mark I received on the entire exam was for misspelling one verb form.

Miss Vega was dumbfounded because my performance was the top in her class, even better than her favorite students who surrounded her in the front of the class. My assigned seat was near the back of the class, maybe because of my height or maybe where the alphabetical lot placed me. Clearly my test scores startled her. She refused to acknowledge my performance and gave me a "C" for that class because she thought I had cheated. She was wrong. I did cheat on exams in high school physics and maybe on one or two other occasions, but not this time. She was wrong, but I didn't confront her uneasiness when I picked up my report card.

Impacted by that grade and my low performance on the Iowa Test, I would have to sit out my year of freshman basketball eligibility at

UCLA. I retook Spanish in UCLA Extension and achieved the "A" grade that I hadn't gotten from Miss Vega.

In college, cheating on exams became a way of getting around putting in the necessary time to earn a grade and I'm not proud of that flaw in my character. It wasn't that I was too tired or didn't have the time to study. The notion of athletes having tutors in college and having others read the text materials and organize them for me to ingest was too much for my immature mind to handle. I took the lazy man's way toward ignorance, under-preparation and underachievement. Mom's **Lesson:** "If you don't do it right the first time, you'll have to lick the cat over." I didn't do it the right way the first time, so do it over again I did. Later on when I was awakened to the fact that I had wasted many years and opportunities to *learn to grow*, I spent the time to learn the information which hadn't changed over the years.

After retiring from professional basketball, I was called by my home town of San Pedro which wanted to honor me by adding my name to its *Walk of Fame*. During the parade down Sixth Street on **Willie Naulls Day**, I saw a somewhat familiar face standing, waving and smiling, "Hello, Willie. Remember me? I'm Miss Vega, your Spanish teacher from high school."

"Of course, Miss Vega, how have you been?" I answered. My inner man jarred my memory bank to recall what it was about this woman that impressed me enough to be cautious at our hand shake. Then I remembered that final exam in the 12th grade as I smiled through the small talk. She introduced me to a couple of her women friends and said she was proud of all that I had accomplished in my life since leaving San Pedro High School. And then she was gone. I didn't get a chance to tell her that I hadn't cheated on her final exam, but maybe that was the right thing. An explanation might have given her the wrong impression of me. *I was a cheater* on exams during the gap between that indelible encounter in high school and the day I saw her at the honoring of my reputation in sports. Mom's **Lesson**: "You can't tell a book by its cover. You have to read inside to find out what's inside." All those years my ego had harbored what I perceived to be an injustice, knowing in my heart that I was a cheater in other classes, even in high school. "The heart is deceitful above all things, and desperately wicked. Who can know it?" (Jeremiah 17:9).

In the ninth grade I played in an Optimist Club basketball tournament in Long Beach, California. A coach from one of our California colleges saw me score 30 or so points in the tournament's championship game. He walked up to me and offered me a scholarship. I didn't even know what he was talking about and told him so. He asked me how old I was and where I went to school. When I told him he was shocked, saying that he thought I'd be a great player some day. But the word "scholarship" and the possibility that someone would pay my way through college if I qualified stuck in my memory. So when I spoke to the high school counselor, Mrs. Suiter, during my mandatory 10th grade session, I had enough information in my mind's store to ask informed questions about which courses were needed to

San Pedro High
School

Physics Class
17 April 1952

Mr. Sawyer,
in the back of the
classroom on the
left, was a very
encouraging teacher.
His son, Don, was
an outstanding
basketball player
at UCLA for
Coach John Wooden.

12th Grade

qualify to receive a college scholarship. Mrs. Suiter, however, encouraged me to major in wood shop. When I imposed upon her my desire to take only college prep courses, she advised me that I should take courses like wood shop to prepare myself to work with my hands. I told her that I was doing enough work with my hands in basketball and baseball. She said, "Oh, well, let's see what you can handle."

When she proposed her first slate of classes, I told her that I had always gotten "A's" in English and I thought *Remedial English* was for people who had either failed English in junior high or for those people who were new to our country. Maybe English was their second language. Mrs. Suiter insisted on putting me on a track that included wood shop as she had evidently made up her mind that I didn't fit the stereotype that she wanted to encourage to prepare for a college experience. Only when I was persistent during our session before my junior year, and after she had reviewed (for the first time) my junior high school transcripts, did she acquiesce to my demand to take the right course load. She assigned me to Mrs. Piggott's college prep English class. I received an "A" grade that semester for my work. Finally my life took a detour away from her contrived tracking of me by the color of my skin.

In retrospect I rarely received academic encouragement in high school or the benefit of empathic, personalized wise counsel. Promoting mental growth of children at every level of development, allowing them to make informed choices that increase options in their lives, should be the agenda of all teachers and counselors. While my experience with this counselor was negative, several of my African American friends who attended Jefferson High School, whose student body was overwhelmingly African American in the '50s, have told me that they received excellent counseling for their college preparation.

Lesson: My mother told me to listen – to hear – before forming questions to find out if someone wished me well. When I listened to Mrs. Suiter, I heard her heart about me. She saw me and didn't care to know me or help me because my skin was Black. I knew she didn't wish me well.

My introduction to Coach John Wooden's basketball program came during my senior year of high school when several alumni, African American professionals including Dr. Davis, Dr. Coleman, Horace Johnson (an administrator with the United States Postal Service), players, former players and friends of UCLA contacted me regarding accepting a scholarship to UCLA. Coach came to my home in Watts once. My mom was greatly impressed and thought him a gentleman, genuinely interested in me as a student athlete. That type of thinking went over my head because I wasn't that thoughtful about academics; I just took it all in.

Playing basketball the way he coached was on my mind since I had first seen UCLA on television. We didn't have a TV in our home at that time, but I remember standing on Pacific Coast Highway in Torrance in front of a local mom and pop store watching UCLA play *fast break* basketball. The little television was mounted inside the store with speakers placed outside the front window pane. The announcer's voice through the small speakers made the game all the more interesting because I had never heard a basketball game announced before. He inspired my interest, allowing me to conjure up my own images – quite in contrast to today's brain influencing, image forming *interpretations* of what is said and seen in the news by lobbying network/cable TV special interest groups.

I enjoyed watching the Bruins because of their fast break style of play. Jerry Norman, Dick Ridgeway, Ronny Livingston, Don Johnson, Barry Porter, Don Bragg, Johnny Moore, Hank Steinman, Ronny Bane, Mike Hibler, Bobby Pounds, Eddy White, et.al., had one common characteristic. They got after the opposition and you'd best bring your lunch when you came to the Sweat Box, the Old Men's Gym. I wanted to experience that.

Coach Wooden was present at all of my City High School Championship tournament games during my senior year. I saw him many times just to the left of the glass backboard in the second deck of the Hollywood High School gym. There he was with his program rolled up when I looked up in the stands from the free throw line. He nodded or waved conspicuously. His point was made clear to me when he told me that he thought I had great potential and if I worked hard I could develop into a fine student athlete. He said UCLA is a wonderful academic institution and that I could receive a fine education there. **The Recruiting Began!**

Eddie Sheldrake of Bruin Basketball had a reputation of being a blue-eyed Mighty Mite of Hoop. I was quite surprised at his shortness and slightness of stature when he picked me up at my home in Watts. After he finally got his car started, he glanced over at me and I at him, and I don't believe either of us was impressed with the other and would have cancelled the recruiting trip then and there had we had a convenient excuse.

The truth in expression allows me to admit that I had been very impressed with the attention given me by alumni of the University of California, Berkeley. There appeared to be a "looser," less rigid atmosphere and attitude of everyone on my visit to the Cal campus up to the north of Oakland where my older sister lived. The players were really pushing me to join them in an NCAA Championship quest. Big Bob McKeen, their All-American center, cagey Bob Matheny, Bob Albo and the Ricksen twins ostensibly wanted me as a teammate and I had made up my mind to accept Cal's offer of an athletic scholarship. No one else knew of my decision, so it wasn't official yet; but I sensed that their overt and very consistent signs of "What will it take, Willie, to get you to come to our school" were genuine and, I might add, very impressive to a young boy from the ghetto.

I had been taught to never accept gifts from strangers or handouts from anyone, but my parents thought it OK to take money for meals and travel to and from college locations during the recruiting phenomenon. So it's with this background of being recruited by highly respected universities that I found myself pushing an old beat up car west on 112th Street and then north up Central Avenue, about five or six blocks from my home, and taking instructions from Eddie. Either he had run out of gas or the car had just gotten tired and stopped. His car sure looked tired. As I looked around me, I realized that God was with us because no one appeared to pay much attention to us, a 6' 6" Black kid pushing this little old car with a 5' 9" bespectacled scrawny White man at the wheel up Central Avenue in Watts, USA. No question about it – I was going to Cal Berkeley.

As the recruiting evening progressed, I found myself at a UCLA Spring Sing, a student production which featured fraternity and sorority group competition in musical presentations and humorous skits, all in joyful anticipation of being crowned Greek house groups of the year. Eddie had departed, probably to revive his car, and the athlete assigned to carry the baton and escort me there was Don Bragg, more of a man in stature than Eddie, and less of a nerdy comedian. This little mighty mite Eddie fellow considered himself a comedian, blurting out wry ego-centric one liners, implying that I was lucky Coach was interested in me, and then laughing more than I did at his own attempts to be humorous. I thought to myself at the time that he not only looked like a donkey eating cactus when he went about his hilarious antics; he acted like one. But to his credit he was consistent. Back to the UCLA Spring Sing . . . .

At my side was Don, a very different per-sonality from Eddie. He was soft-spoken, yet clear-ly understood. He appeared to be interested in me, Willie, and not just the jock Willie; or at least that was my first impression, which we all know is often lasting. There was a John Wooden Spirit which moved upon our presence and engaged my mind as I sat there with Don laughing; and I found myself in a healthy state of reconsidering yet again my first impression of UCLA which had considered Coach Wooden and his program as my first choice. As Don dropped me off in Watts later that night, my veins were filled with Blue-and-Gold blood and I was then and there, forever more, a UCLA Bruin.

Eddie and Don contributed to the rich tradition of UCLA basketball which inspires a real study in diversity. In the Wooden tradition, we came to his boot camp from a variety of socio-economic backgrounds and circumstances and left the University filled with enough knowledge to know how to coexist and succeed and grow toward fulfilling God's intent for our lives. We learned that success in life was up to us, individually. That knowledge infusion was in fact a transfusion in thinking offered to all of us. All Hope and Truth and Life come from God. He offers His Wisdom through His ministers at every station He builds. Coach Wooden, a minister and wise counselor, continues His God-given mission work even today in words and deeds. Without Coach's supervision and input into my life, I believe that I would have had a different, more commonly traveled, journey.

Following graduation from high school, I looked forward eagerly to attending UCLA and playing basketball on Coach John Wooden's Bruin team. The second volume of *Levitation's View: Lessons Voiced from an Extraordinary Journey* will chronicle my experience as an integral part of the integration of Westwood Village and Coach Wooden's forming basketball dynasty at UCLA.

Volume II: The Wooden Years will be available in 2005.

Courtesy of *The Los Angeles Examiner* • 9 March 1956

This cartoon could imply that Coach Twogood of USC had the power of "white magic" to bespell jumping ability into the legs of his players on his all-White team.

ONLY GOD GIVES GIFTS TO WHOMEVER HE CHOOSES.

Every Child's Primal Scream:
"Do You Wish Me Well?"

Do you wish me well?
'cause it's hard to tell
Don't see me in the life you sell
so it's hard to tell
Do you wish me well?

Do you wish me well?
Or do you just try to see
what you can get out of me
off my fruit bearing tree
It's hard to tell
Do you wish me well?

Do you wish me well?
Or am I to be
a mining pan for thee
for your kids to see
how to exploit the free
talent God gave me
Do you wish me well?

Do you wish me well?
What a stand to make
for truth in living sake
don't know how to break
it down more, for your sake
Do you wish me well?

Do you wish me well?
In your eyes I see
insincerity's tree
you don't wanna be
deep in love with me, so
it's hard to tell
Do you wish me well?

Do you wish me well?
'cause it's hard to tell
by the stuff you sell
with your mouth as well
words straight out of hell
Do you wish me well?
Do you wish me well?
Do you wish me well?

Do you wish me well?
'cause I'm saved like you
in all that we do
we're in the same pool too
like being a Jew
only God foreknew
I'm unique like you
Yeah, an individual too
Do you wish me well?
Do you wish me well?
Do you wish me well?

Do you wish me well?
'cause it's hard to tell
by the route you walk
and the commitment you talk
challenging my freedom to be
sharing Christ – as THE
Eternal Hope in me
for the world to see
Do you wish me well?
Do you wish me well?

Do you wish me well?
Makes no difference now
for I've learned to tell
how the Master's plan
wills that I wish you well
so that's what I sell
check your heart to know
Do you wish me well?